SAIGON
CALLING

MARCELINO TRUONG

SAIGON CALLING

LONDON 1963-75

Translated by David Homel

PLOINK
PLOINK

ARSENAL PULP PRESS
Vancouver

SAIGON CALLING: London 1963-75
by Marcelino Truong
English-language translation copyright © 2017 by David Homel

First published in French as *Give Peace a Chance: Londres 1963-75*
© 2015 Editions Denoël

ARSENAL PULP PRESS
Suite 202 - 211 East Georgia St.
Vancouver, BC V6A 1Z6
Canada
arsenalpulp.com

This book has received support from the Institut français' Publication Support Programmes. Cet ouvrage a bénéficié du soutien des Programmes d'aide à la publication de l'Institut français.

Liberté • Égalité • Fraternité
RÉPUBLIQUE FRANÇAISE

The publisher gratefully acknowledges the support of the Government of Canada and the Government of British Columbia (through the Book Publishing Tax Credit Program) for its publishing activities.

Canada

Editing of translation by Brian Lam
Design of translated edition by by Oliver McPartlin
Original design by Les Associés Réunis

Printed and bound in Canada

Library and Archives Canada Cataloguing in Publication:
Truong, Marcelino
[Give peace a chance. English]
        Saigon calling : London, 1963-75 / Marcelino Truong ; David
Homel, translator.

Translation of the original French book issued under English title: Give peace a chance.
Issued in print and electronic formats.
ISBN 978-1-55152-689-8 (softcover).--ISBN 978-1-55152-690-4 (HTML).--
ISBN 978-1-55152-691-1 (PDF)

    1. Truong, Marcelino--Comic books, strips, etc. 2. Truong, Marcelino--Childhood--Comic books, strips, etc. 3. Truong, Marcelino--Family--Comic books, strips, etc. 4. London (England)--History--1951- --Comic books, strips, etc. 5. Vietnamese--Great Britain--Comic books, strips, etc. 6. Vietnam War, 1961-1975--Personal narratives, Vietnamese--Comic books, strips, etc. 7. Autobiographical comics. I. Homel, David, translator II. Title. III. Title: Give peace a chance. English

DA676.8.T78A3 2017   942.1'2004959220092   C2017-903941-5
                                                          C2017-903942-3

When we forgive, we benefit from the forgiveness, for we then cease to
bear the weight of resentment.

But still, we must never accept that an injustice be repeated.

—Buddha

A RUMOR IN THE WIND

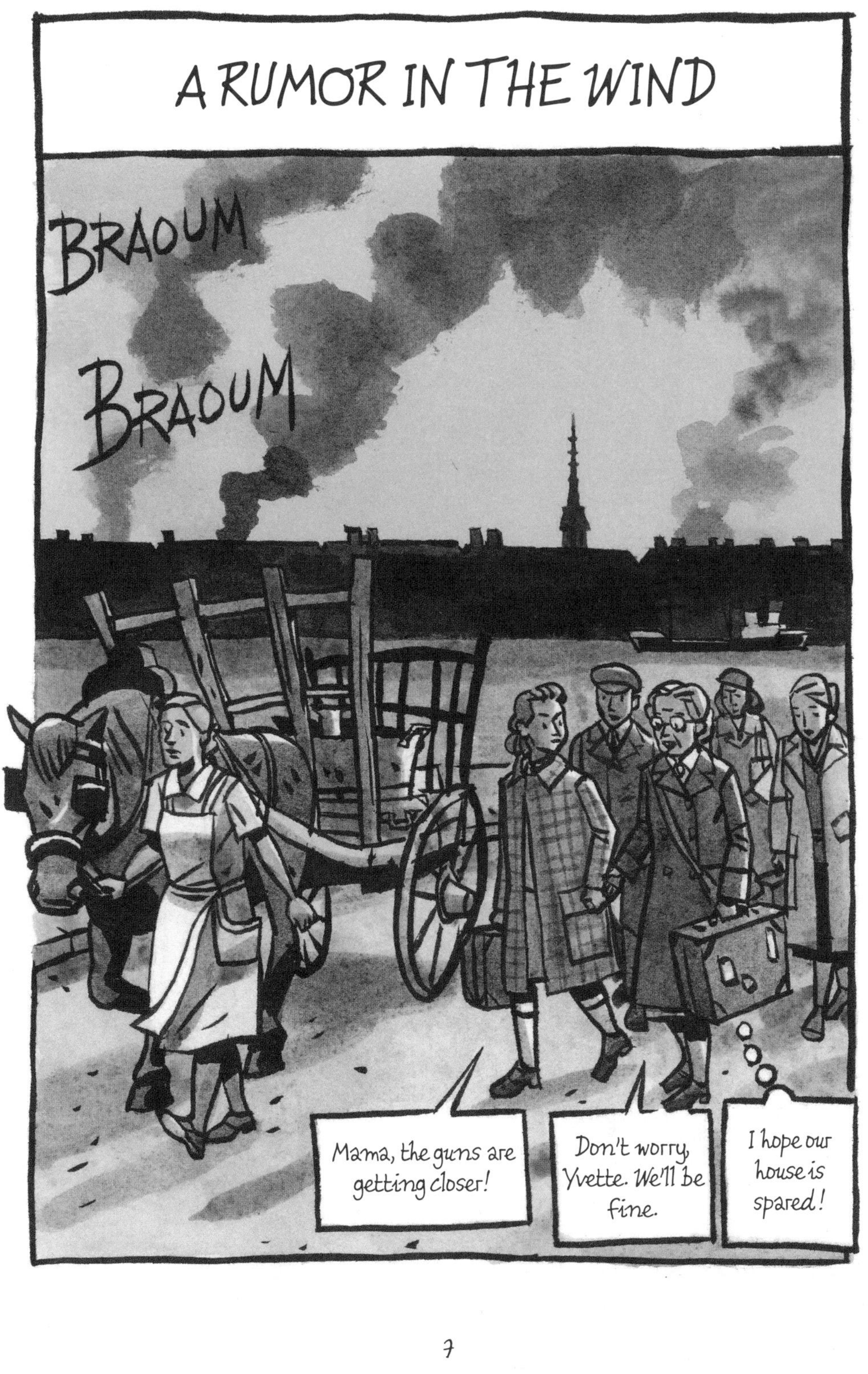
BRAOUM
BRAOUM
Mama, the guns are getting closer!
Don't worry, Yvette. We'll be fine.
I hope our house is spared!

Saint-Malo, August 1944. The battle for the liberation of France was raging. The Germans ordered the fortified city be evacuated. The population tried to find some refuge in the back country. My mother and grandmother were part of the exodus.

*Blend in with the civilians! *Right away, lieutenant!

9

* Watch out! Yankee Mustangs!

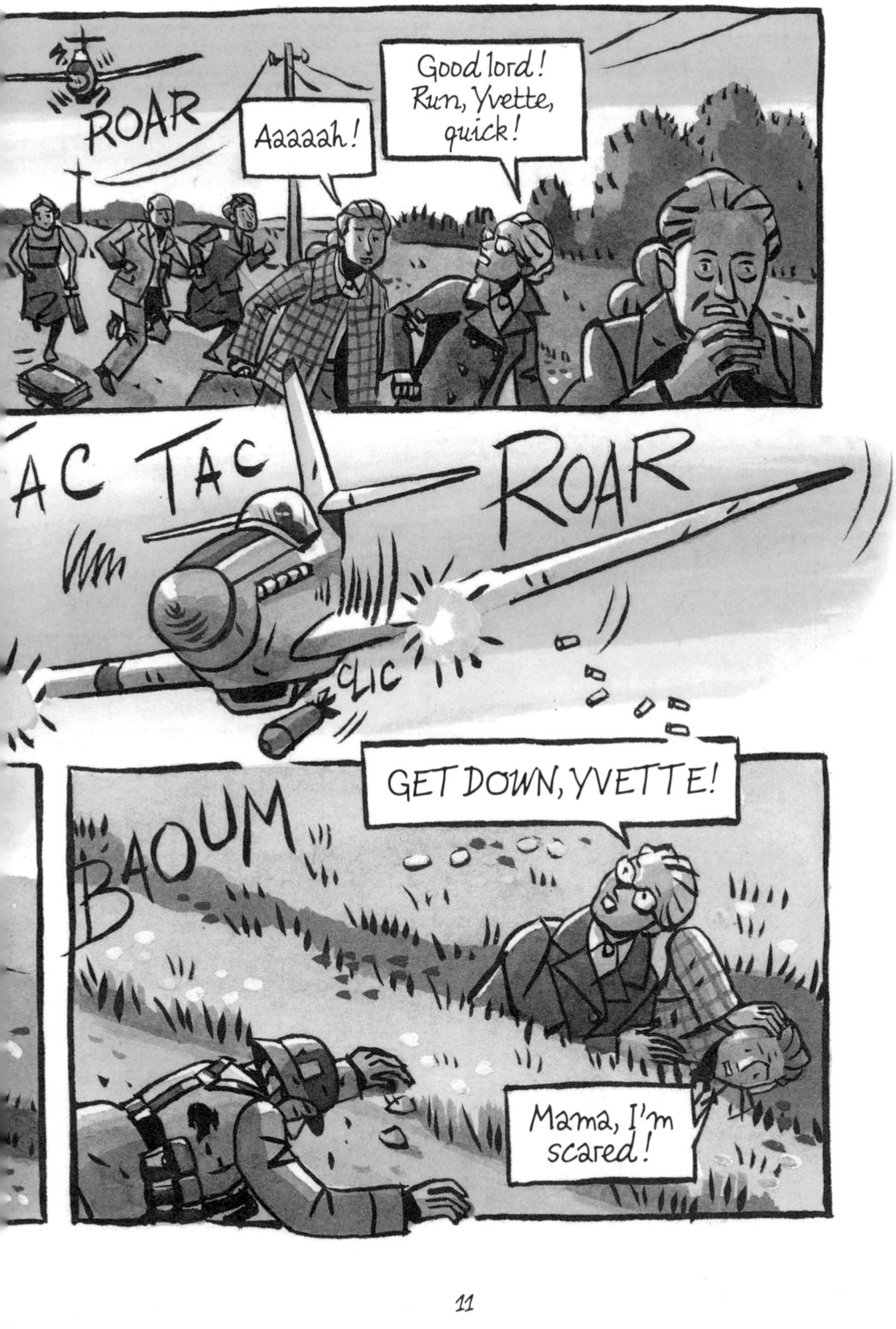
ROAR
Aaaaah!
Good lord! Run, Yvette, quick!
AC TAC
ROAR
CLIC
BAOUM
GET DOWN, YVETTE!
Mama, I'm scared!

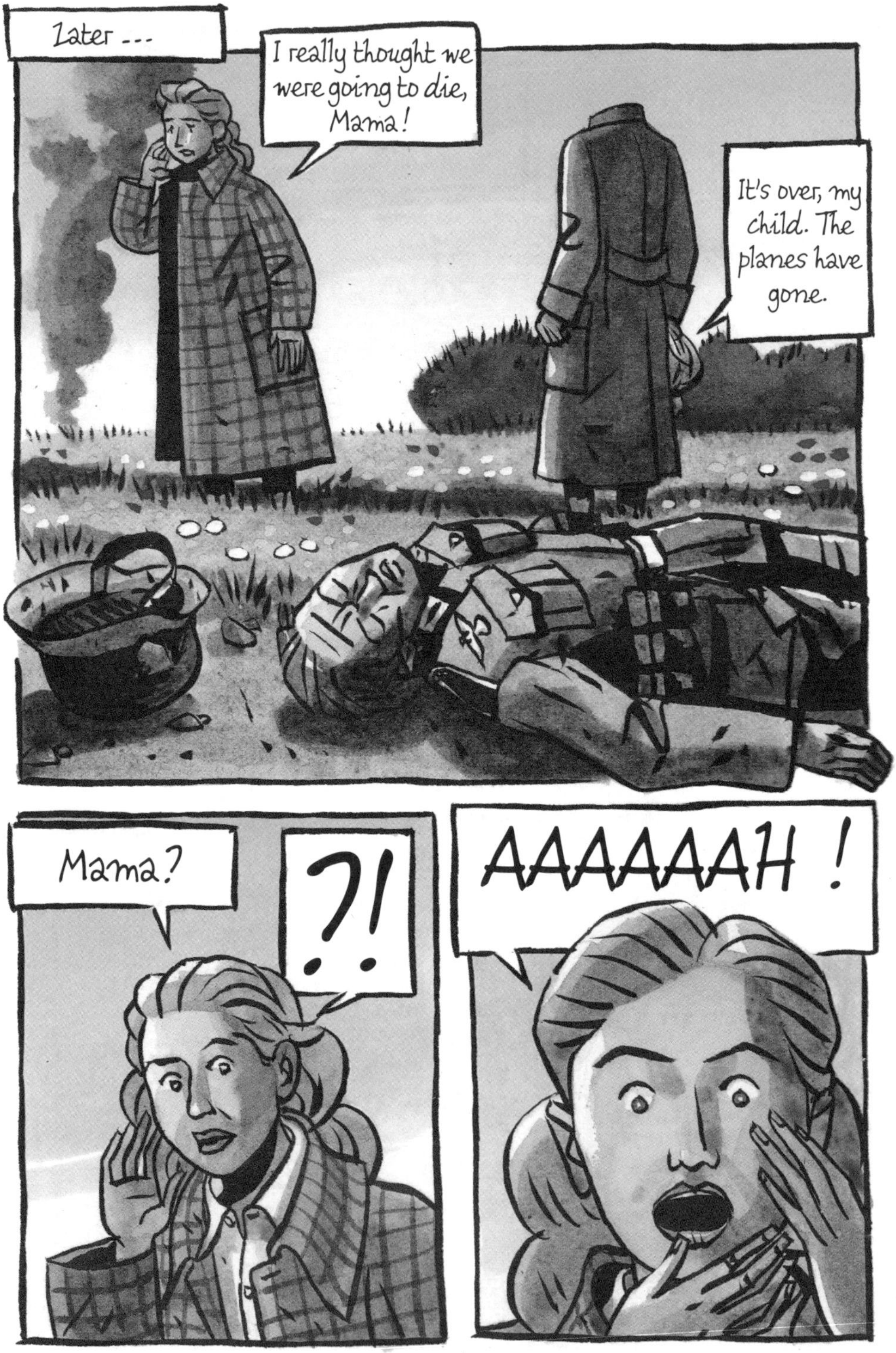
Later ...
I really thought we were going to die, Mama!
It's over, my child. The planes have gone.
Mama?
?!
AAAAAAH !

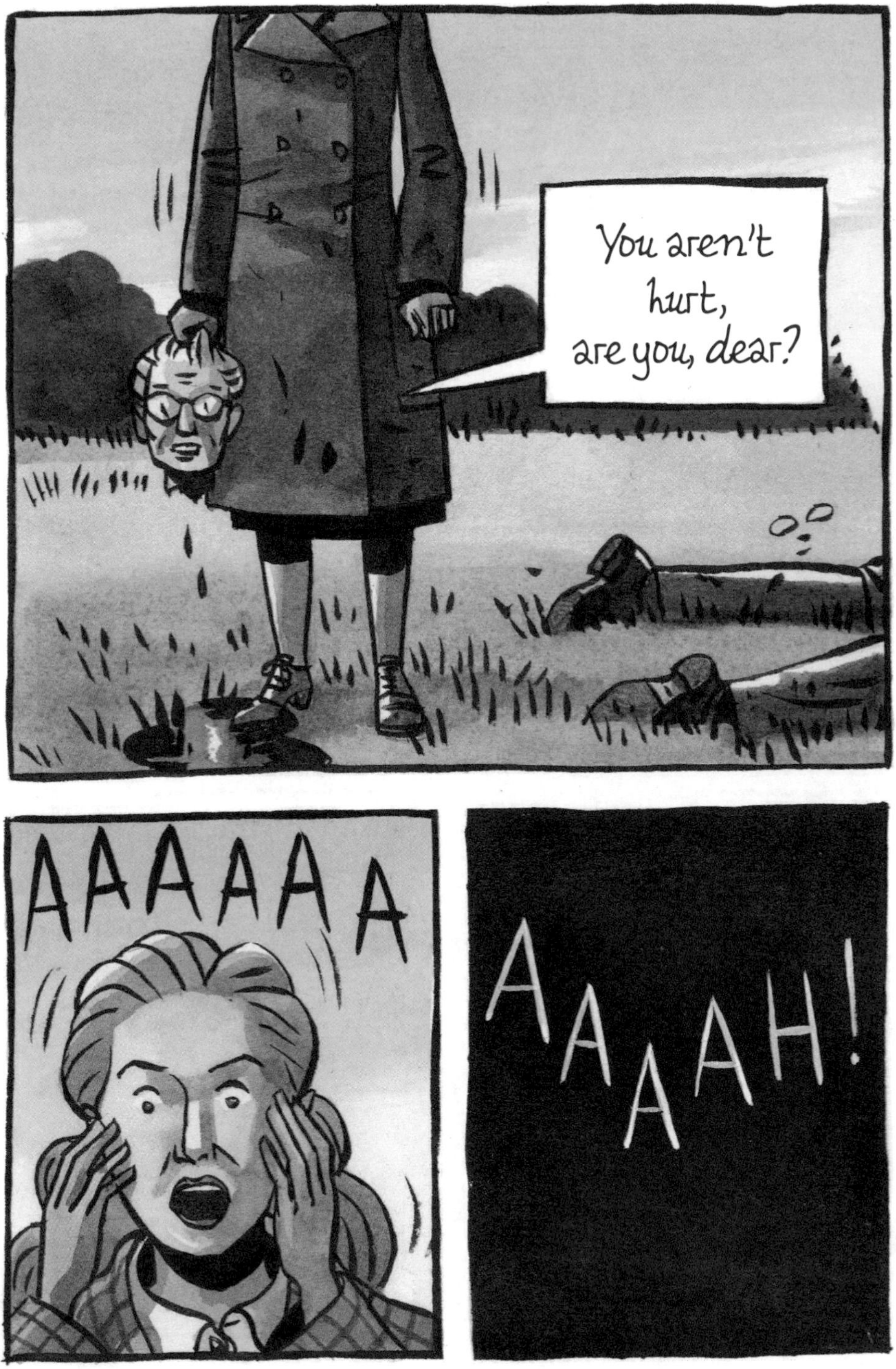
You aren't hurt, are you, dear?
AAAAAA
AAAAH!

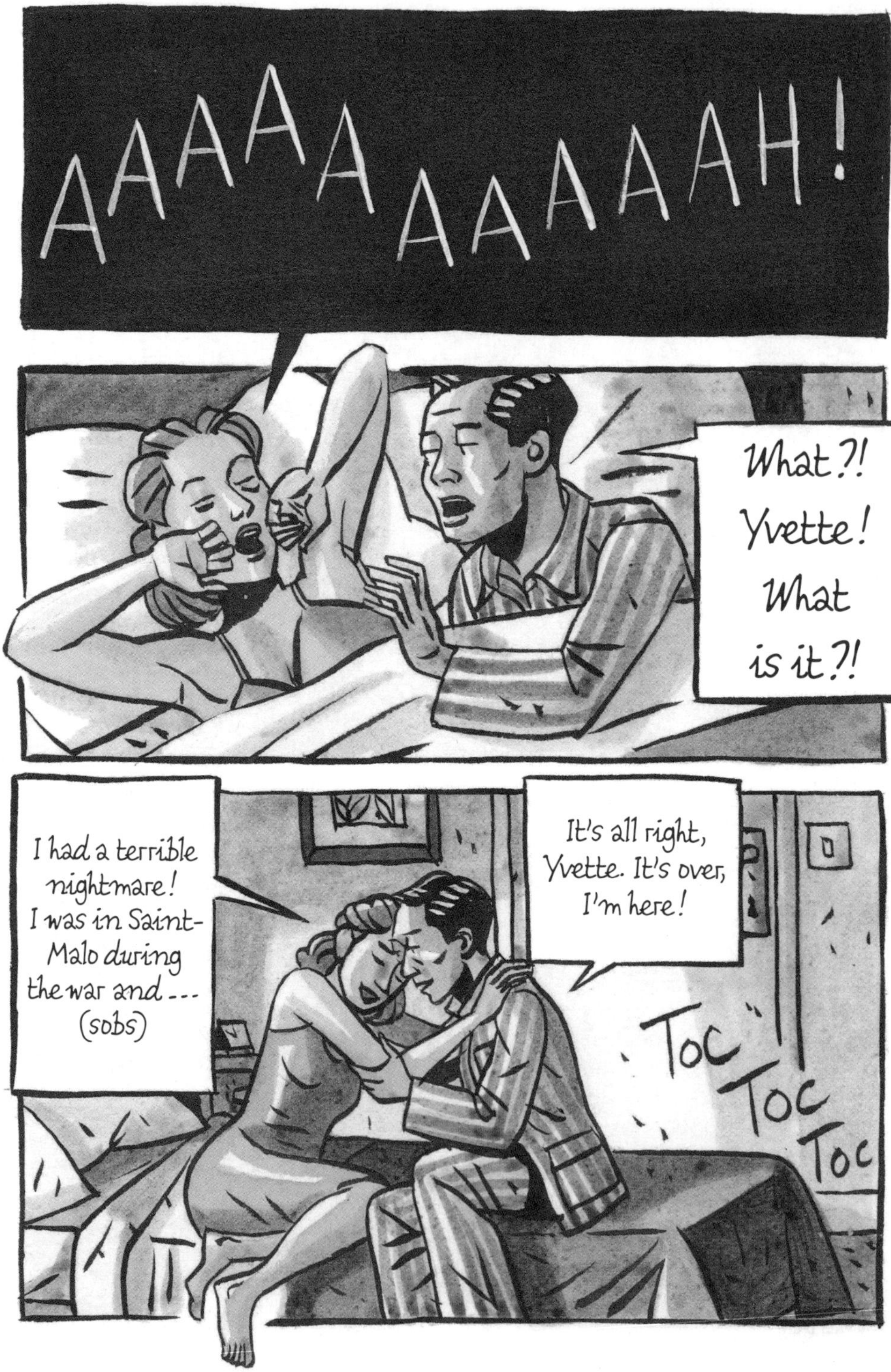
AAAAAAAAAAAH!
What?! Yvette! What is it?!
I had a terrible nightmare! I was in Saint-Malo during the war and ... (sobs)
It's all right, Yvette. It's over, I'm here!
Toc Toc Toc

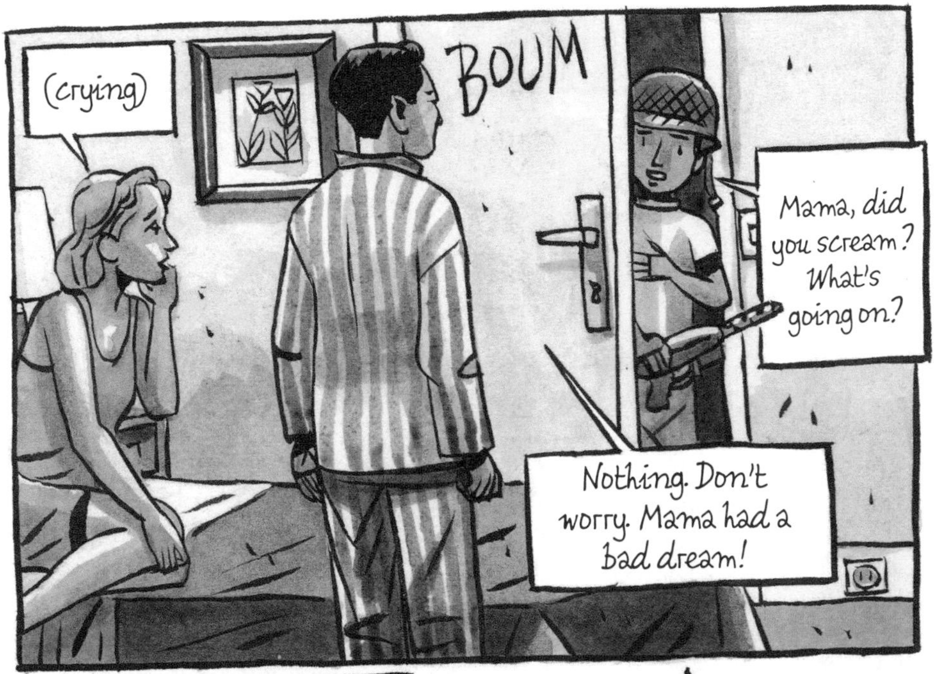
(crying)
BOUM
Mama, did you scream? What's going on?
Nothing. Don't worry. Mama had a bad dream!

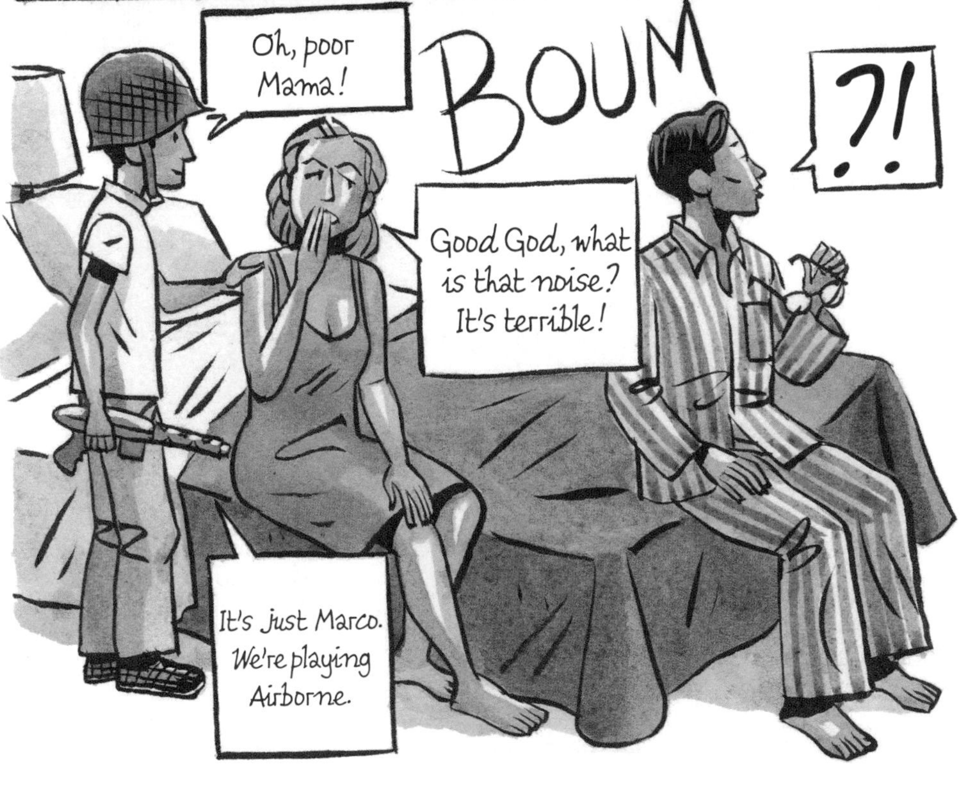
Oh, poor Mama!
BOUM
?!
Good God, what is that noise? It's terrible!
It's just Marco. We're playing Airborne.

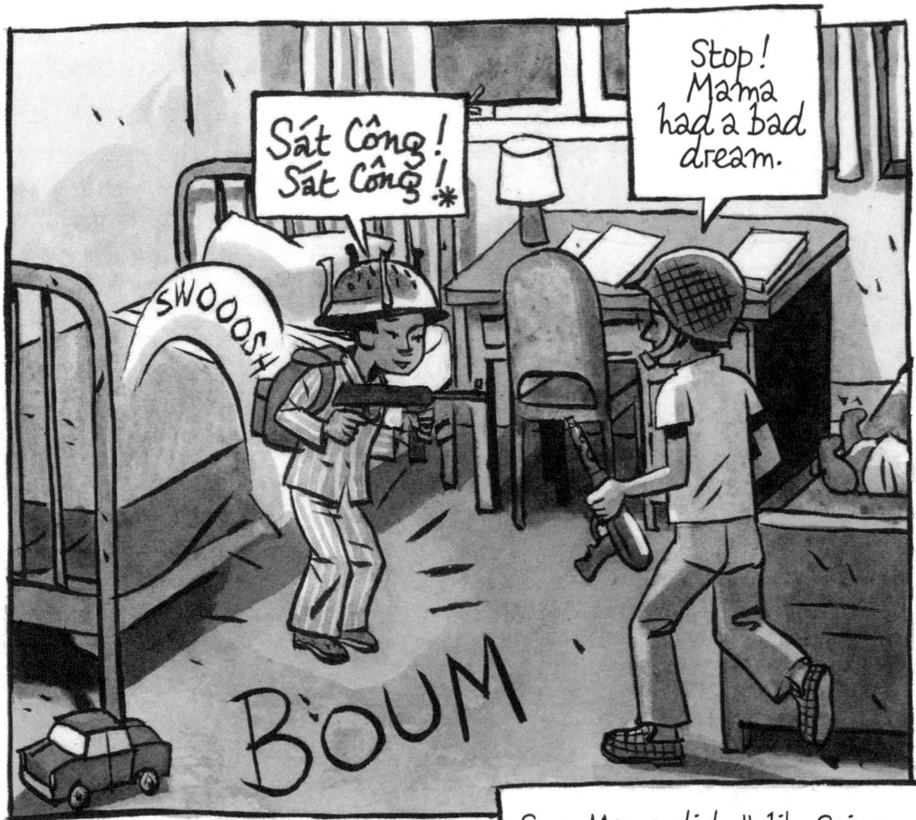
Sát Công! Sát Công!*
Stop! Mama had a bad dream.
SWOOOSH
BOUM

* Kill the Commies!

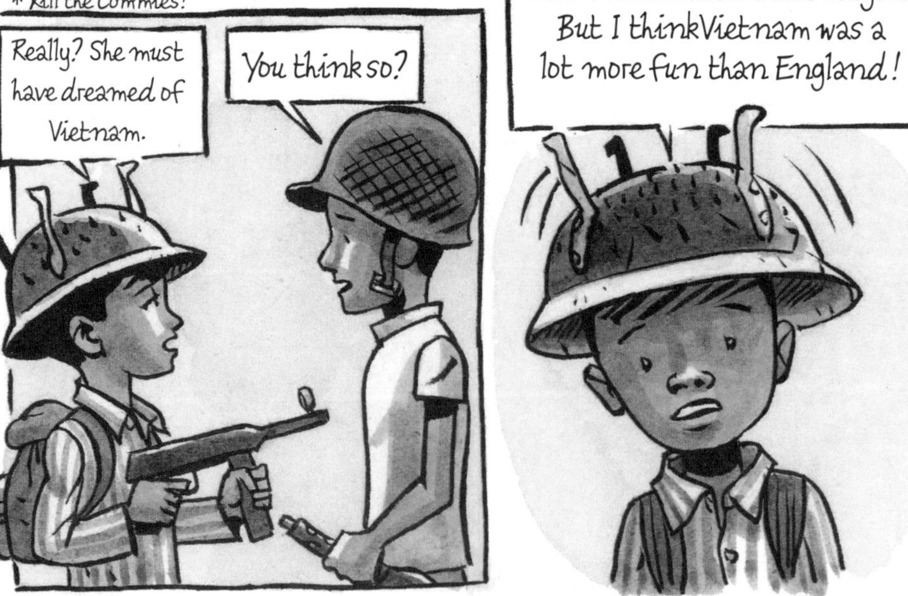
Really? She must have dreamed of Vietnam.
You think so?
Sure. Mama didn't like Saigon. But I think Vietnam was a lot more fun than England!

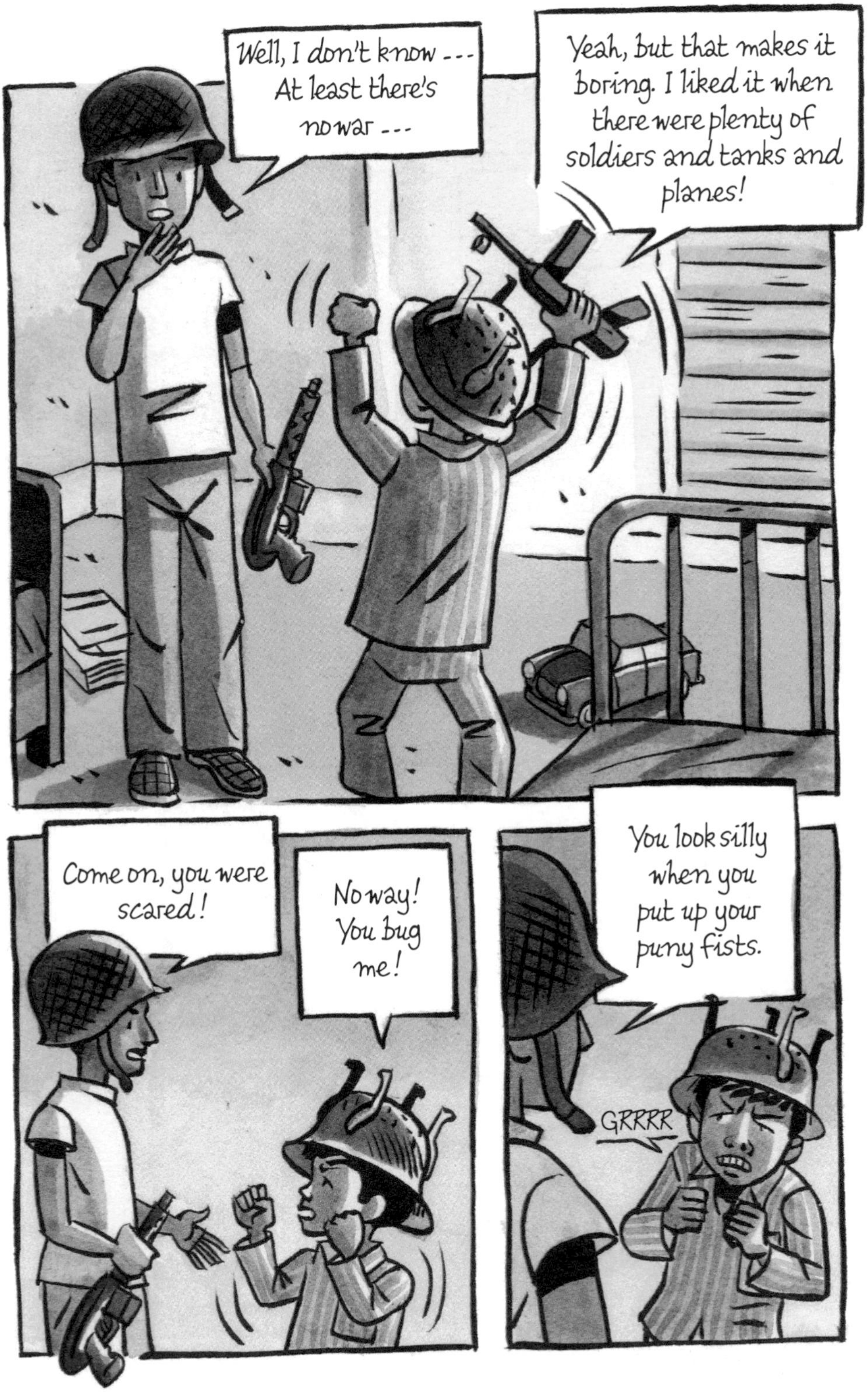
Well, I don't know --- At least there's no war ---
Yeah, but that makes it boring. I liked it when there were plenty of soldiers and tanks and planes!
Come on, you were scared!
No way! You bug me!
You look silly when you put up your puny fists.
GRRRR

* My sister and brother used that nickname to torture me.

18

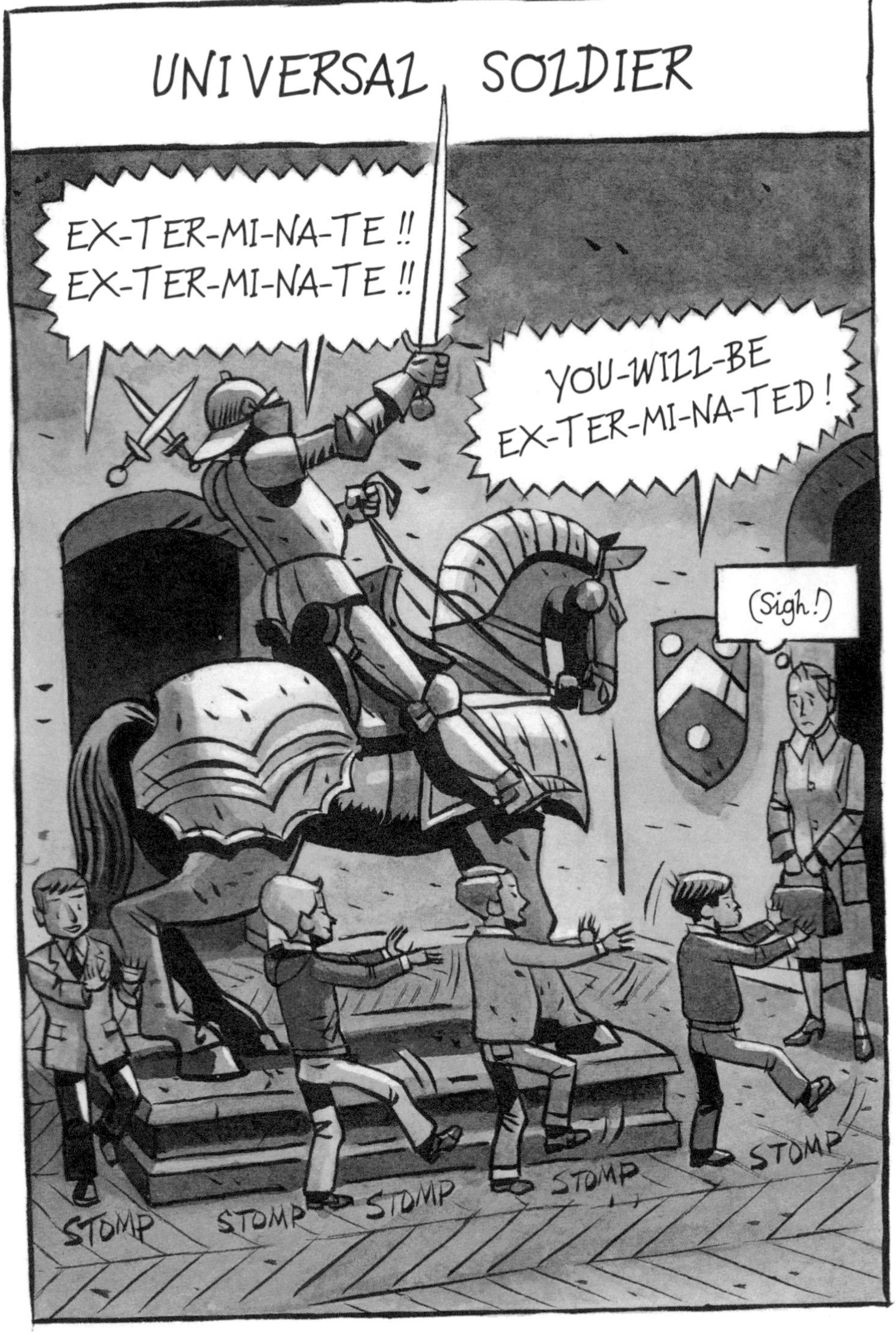
UNIVERSAL SOLDIER
EX-TER-MI-NA-TE !! EX-TER-MI-NA-TE !!
YOU-WILL-BE EX-TER-MI-NA-TED !
(Sigh!)
STOMP
STOMP
STOMP
STOMP
STOMP

London in 1963 and 1964 was very different from Saigon. We had moved from tropical heat to smog, from noisy crowds to quiet

streets, from Asian anarchy to British manners and that stiff upper lip of theirs. Strangely, I remember less about our arrival in London

an our two colorful years in Saigon. The "Pax Britannica" seemed rather ·ab after our distant, exotic Asian war ---

Papa was a counselor (No. 2) at the Vietnamese embassy. I remember once when he rented a fancy coat and tails to accompany Ambassador Vu Van Mau* who was to present his credentials to Queen Elizabeth II.

*Vu Van Mau replaced Ngô Dinh Luyên, the brother of President Ngô Dinh Diêm, assassinated November 2, 1963.

We discovered the wonders of British television and its legendary series: Danger Man, The Avengers, Doctor Who, etc... I can still hear the Kraftwerk-style credits music of Doctor Who that imitated a strange instrument called the theremin.

Every Thursday, we watched the new show on the BBC: Top of the Pops!!

For my seventh birthday, I invited my friends from the French Lycée and Mama took us to the Tower of London.

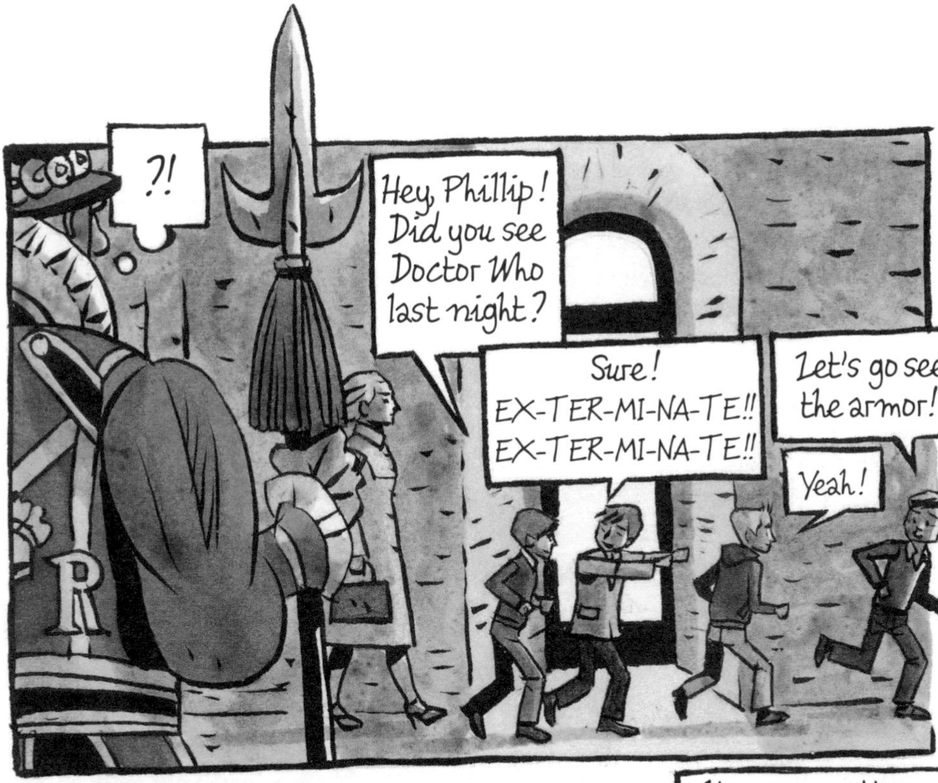
?!
Hey, Phillip! Did you see Doctor Who last night?
Sure! EX-TER-MI-NA-TE!! EX-TER-MI-NA-TE!!
Let's go see the armor!
Yeah!

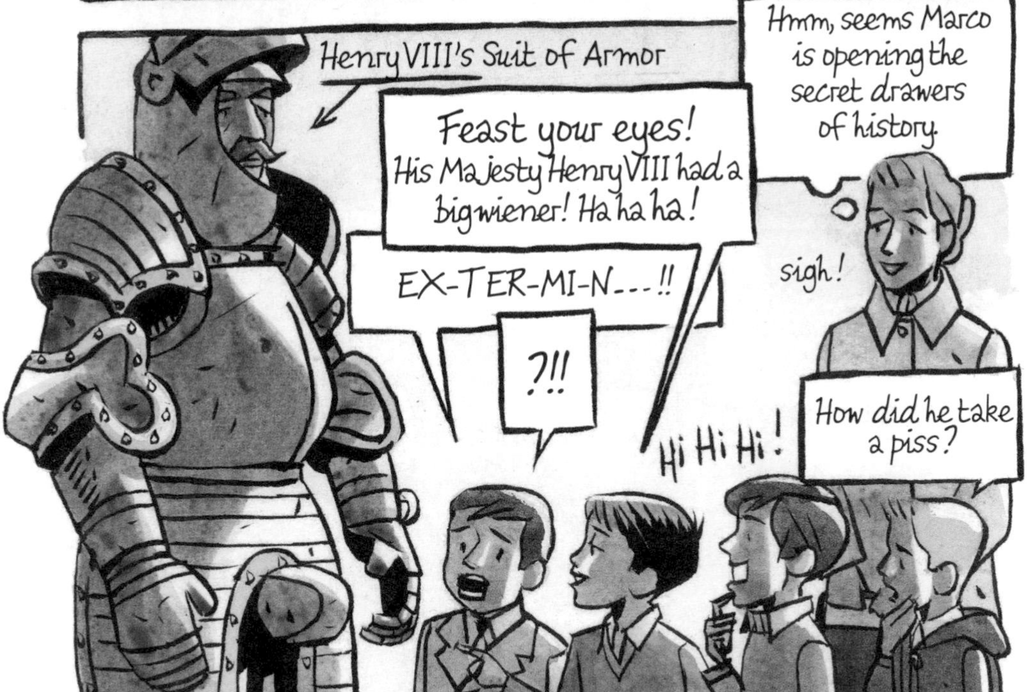
Henry VIII's Suit of Armor
Hmm, seems Marco is opening the secret drawers of history.
Feast your eyes! His Majesty Henry VIII had a big wiener! Ha ha ha!
EX-TER-MI-N---!!
sigh!
?!!
How did he take a piss?
Hi Hi Hi!

Like the British, we turned into TV addicts. Vietnam was often in the news.

An American aircraft-carrier, the USS CARD, was sunk in Saigon harbour by an explosive charge placed by communist terrorists.*

Can't be true!

What's he saying?

The Viêt-Cong sank an American aircraft carrier in Saigon.

It looks like the aircraft carrier I saw!

Shhh!

I missed it all.

They said the ship was loaded with helicopters to fight the Viêt-Cong guerrillas.

*May, 1964

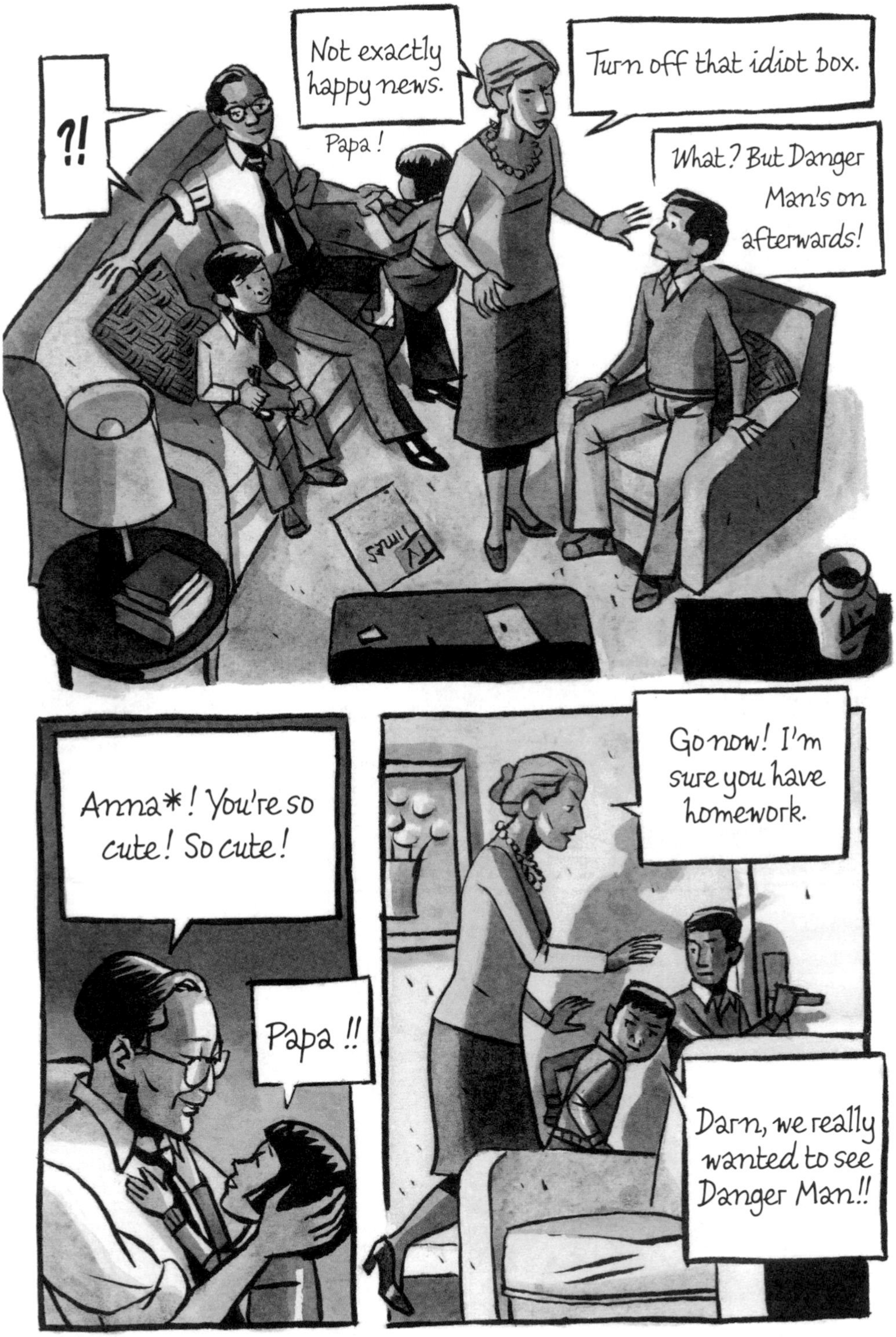
?!
Not exactly happy news.
Papa!
Turn off that idiot box.
What? But Danger Man's on afterwards!
TV times
Anna*! You're so cute! So cute!
Papa!!
Go now! I'm sure you have homework.
Darn, we really wanted to see Danger Man!!

* Anh-Noëlle's nickname.

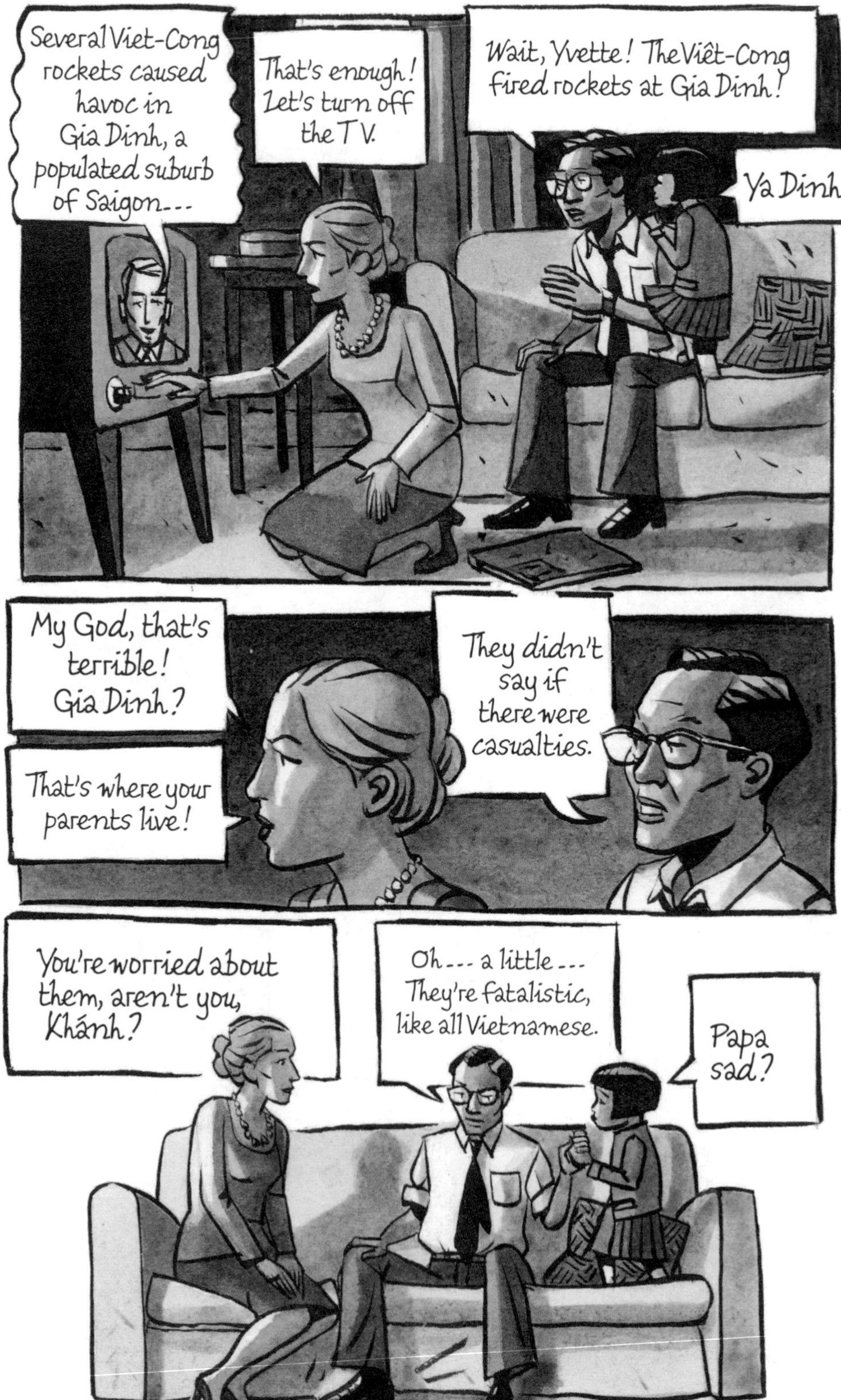

Several Viet-Cong rockets caused havoc in Gia Dinh, a populated suburb of Saigon...
That's enough! Let's turn off the T.V.
Wait, Yvette! The Viêt-Cong fired rockets at Gia Dinh!
Ya Dinh!
My God, that's terrible! Gia Dinh?
That's where your parents live!
They didn't say if there were casualties.
You're worried about them, aren't you, Khánh?
Oh... a little... They're fatalistic, like all Vietnamese.
Papa sad?

PAPER TIGER*

McNamara, American Secretary of Defense, six-foot-three

General Nguyễn Khánh, Prime Minister, five-foot-three

General Taylor, Chairman of the American Joint Chiefs of Staff, six-foot-five

See that? With his arms in the air, General Khánh looks just like a puppet!

PEACE, YES! PEKING, NO!

McNAMARA'S RIGHT. LET'S FIGHT!

CLAP CLAP CLAP

* "All reactionaries are paper tigers." —Mao Zedong

Chaos had ruled ever since the 1963 putsch and the assassination of President Diêm. It was a merry-go-round of generals, like a game of musical chairs. Street demonstrations broke out daily.

When General Khánh managed to take over in 1964, he made the cover of Time magazine.

I remember Papa's consternation ...

Who's the soldier with the billy-goat beard?

That's just General Khánh

Saigon's strongman of the month ...

He's a little plump to be an Airborne.

Wow! That's a Viêt-Cong flag. And a US M1 rifle!

All in bad taste, I'm afraid.

A shameful image for South Vietnam. We look like some Latin American banana republic!

Papa played the role of ambassador until a new South Vietnamese representative could be named. I remember a reception commemorating the partition of the country ten years earlier. Papa gave a speech in Vietnamese.

* The Republic of Vietnam wants to live in peace behind the shelter of the 17th parallel!

31

Taking advantage of the political instability in Saigon, Hanoi stepped up the shipments of men and weapons into the South via the Hô Chi Minh Trail.

Six to eight weeks of marching, and we'll liberate the South from the corrupt clique of puppets.

The Communist guerrillas in the South, backed by the North Vietnamese, were a real threat to the soldiers of the Saigon regime.

Shit, I've got a brother, his outpost was overrun by a Viêt-Cong attack. Not a single survivor!

Yeah, they're getting stronger. And our bosses hang out in Saigon and line their pockets with American dollars!

Too busy jousting for power, the generals and colonels neglected their duties. The lack of effort exasperated American military advisors and diplomats.

In 1964, President Lyndon B. Johnson sent his Secretary of Defense Bob McNamara to South Vietnam. McNamara was a winner who'd set things straight. He even tried to say a few words in Vietnamese ---

Seconded by General Taylor, McNamara the giant went on tour with General Khánh. The two Americans ended every speech by grabbing the diminutive soldier's hands and raising them in the "V for victory" sign. The result: General Khánh looked just like a puppet ---

* Long live Vietnam!

General Khánh and the Young Turks of his entourage managed to convince the Americans that they had to bring the war to North Vietnam.

A secret sabotage and intelligence operation was launched north of the 17th parallel, the dividing line between the two Vietnams.

The South Vietnamese raid failed, but it produced an unexpected benefit. Washington claimed that an American destroyer supporting the commando operation was attacked by North Vietnamese gunboats.

The incident gave Johnson ammunition. He charged the North with aggression, and convinced Congress to vote in the Gulf of Tonkin Resolution in August 1964. It gave LBJ carte blanche to involve his country further in the Vietnamese conflict, which he did while claiming not to.

One of LBJ's first acts was to order the bombing of North Vietnamese targets.

The Viêt-Cong responded to the strikes by hitting American air bases in the South.

So LBJ decided to put troops on the ground...

Those Reds are attacking our boys! I'm sending in the Marines, General!

... and get involved whole-hog. In 1965, he sent a large-scale contingent of Marines to shore up Vietnam.

Two years later, as a result of this escalation, there were more than 600,000 GIs south of the 17th parallel.

From 1965 on, the Vietnam War gradually became the monstrous conflict that lasted until 1975.

The Americans carried out the war on a large and small scale. They combined massive bombing in the North and South...

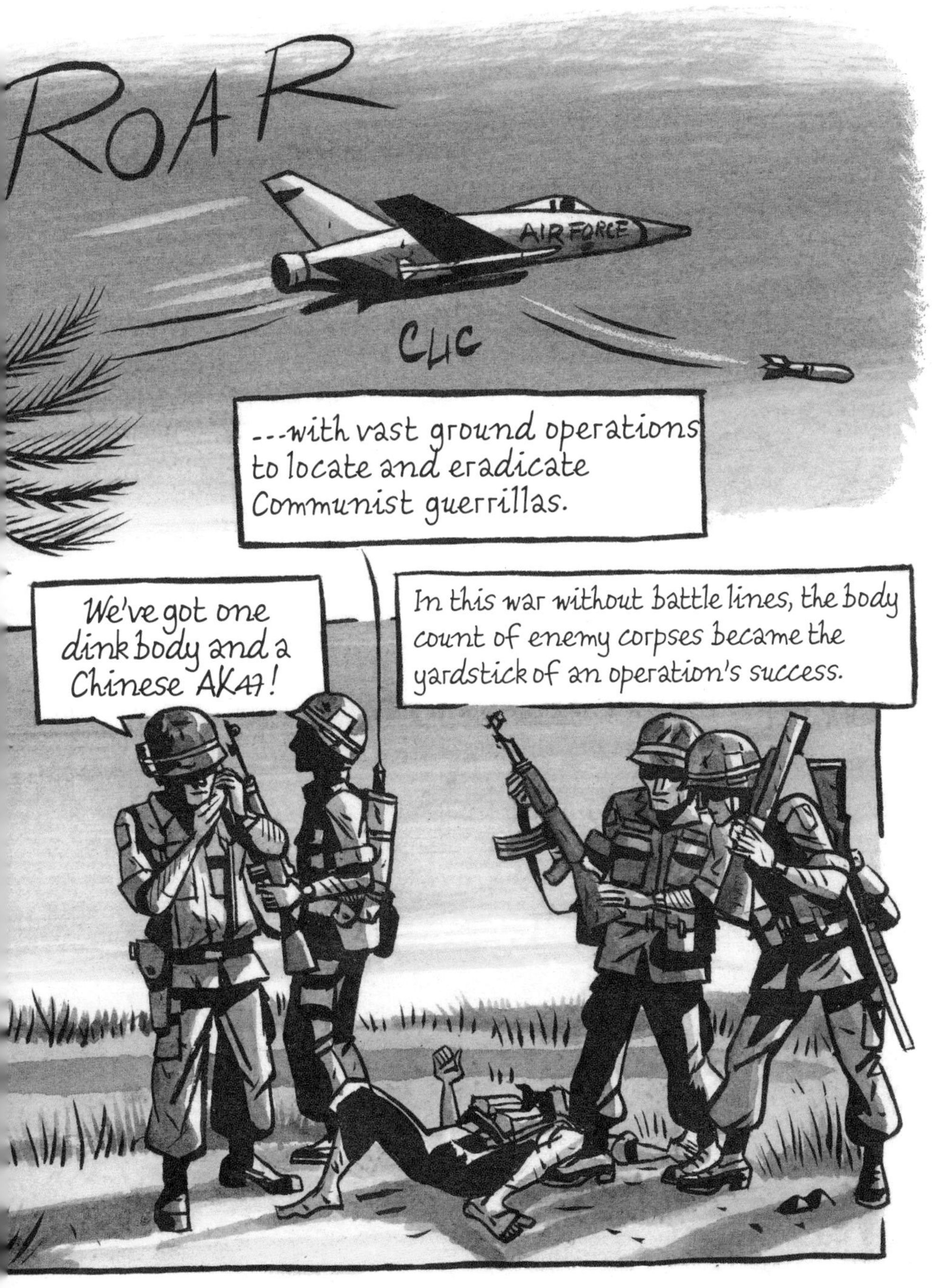
ROAR
AIR FORCE
CLIC
---with vast ground operations to locate and eradicate Communist guerrillas.
We've got one dink body and a Chinese AK47!
In this war without battle lines, the body count of enemy corpses became the yardstick of an operation's success.

The guerrillas live among the peasantry the way fish live in the water, according to Mao Zedong. During the Vietnam War, the Communist guerrillas

In revolutionary warfare, the population is one of the major objectives. Hearts and minds must be cajoled or conquered. Courted one day and

blended into the rural population that had no choice but to accept them. The peasants were soon exposed to massive American attack.

thrashed the next, the peasants paid a high price to soldiers on both sides.

* I hate the clique of Saigon puppets!

South Vietnamese society was shaken by this storm of violence. Fleeing the fighting in the countryside, streams of refugees poured

Around the world, the Vietnam War became ever more unpopular.

into the cities where prostitution and other illegal activities flourished.

*OK, cool ?

Demonstrators painted the Saigon regime as a puppet state, and the massive presence of the US military in the South seemed to confirm that.

The Saigon "puppets" felt the same way about their Communist enemies, as this tract produced by their psychological warfare division shows. These leaflets were dropped by the thousands over zones controlled by the Viêt-Cong. This one from 1965 shows Mao arming the North Vietnamese water buffalo and donkey, who march off to spread terror in the South, while China bags the North's rice crop.

Red China's influence on North Vietnam might have been less visible, but it was just as real.

We were aware of the indignation caused by the Vietnam War. At age 13, our sister loved to sing Dylan and Baez songs.

How can America drop bombs on babies?

Yuk! I can't stand Joan Bizz (sic). Too sticky-sweet!

Mireille sings that song with the French Girl Guides!

Papa, my friends ask me why the Americans are in Vietnam ---

They're helping South Vietnam defend itself ---

Can't the South Vietnamese get along on their own?

South Vietnam is too weak to fight the Communists ---

But all that violence --- It's shameful!

--- Well...

It's the price we pay for freedom.

Look at Europe! Would they have beaten the Nazis without the Americans' help?

He must have sensed how things would turn out. A year after we arrived in London, Papa decided to quit the Vietnam Embassy ---

And I once dreamed of real democracy in Vietnam, with a majority government, an opposition, elections ---

Instead, we have a military regime in the South, and a Stalinist dictatorship in the North ---

Yvette could never return to a country at war ---

The kids will have better schooling in Europe ---

I HAVE TO FIND ANOTHER JOB ---

* "Chanson pour l'Auvergnat," Georges Brassens, 1954

At the end of 1964, thanks to a British correspondent working at the Reuters news agency, whom he had met in Saigon, Papa got a break.

The director of Reuters is going to give me a chance.

I'm sure you'll make a good impression!

MIND THE GAP!

The children will study in peace and quiet at the French Lycée, then Oxford or Cambridge.

?!

VRRRRR

Well, they'll have to put their shoulders to the wheel.

They'll have ideal conditions for their studies!

Will Domi make the grade....?

Papa was recruited by the French desk at Reuters to translate news releases from English to French. Often he was entrusted with the night shift at the headquarters on Fleet Street.

Happy Christmas, Mr Khánh! Fancy a cuppa?

Oh! Happy Christmas, John! Yes, with sugar please.

TCHIK TCHIK TCHIK

The night before Christmas in Saigon, the explosion of two booby-trapped vehicles under the downtown Brinks Hotel, where American officers were billeted, resulted in two Americans dead and dozens wounded. The attack was carefully planned down to the second ...

TCHIK TCHIKTCHIK TCHIK

--- and carried out by --- Viêt-Cong agents --- wearing --- regulation --- army uniforms ---

Damn! I just hope my parents are all right!

TCHIK TCHIK

My father quickly took to his new job, but it brought in much less than his post at the embassy. He had to find other sources of income.

Despite resigning, Papa received a very tempting offer.

The time came to leave South Kensington for a cheaper apartment in the southern suburb of Wimbledon.

I hope my friends will want to come this far.

They will! People are used to traveling in London.

WOODSIDE HOUSE

♩♪ And now, the FAB FOUR from Liverpool! Those lovable MOP-TOPS ♫

boxes to empty! miss the lively center...

Wimbledon is far from the center and the French Lycée, but the children will be able to run wild in the park, the "Common". The boys do wear me out! Young people in England put on such hoodlum airs!

VIM

VIM

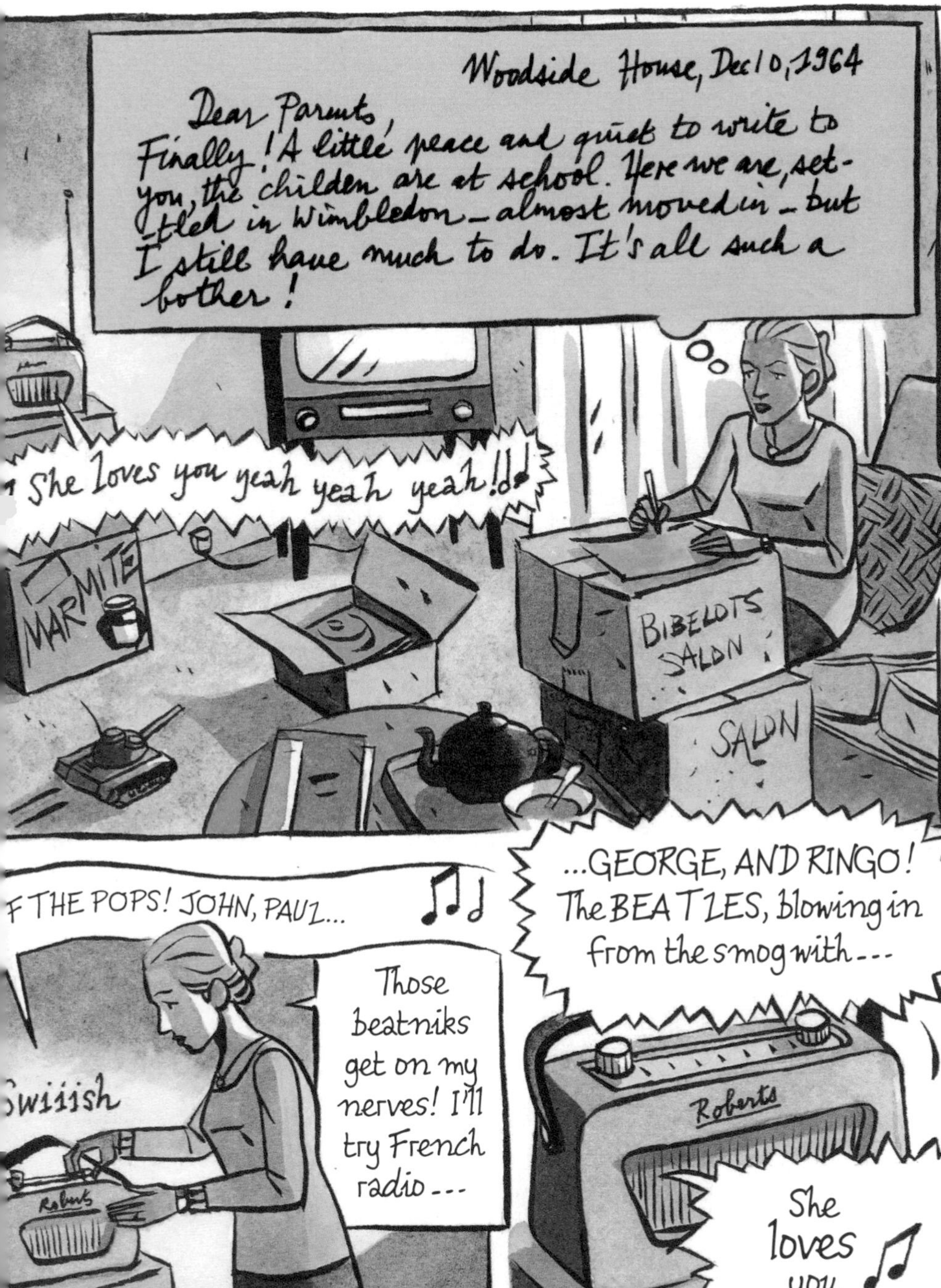
Woodside House, Dec 10, 1964
Dear Parents,
Finally! A little peace and quiet to write to you, the children are at school. Here we are, set-tled in Wimbledon — almost moved in — but I still have much to do. It's all such a bother!
She loves you yeah yeah yeah!
MARMITE
BIBELOTS SALON
SALON
F THE POPS! JOHN, PAUL...
...GEORGE, AND RINGO! The BEATLES, blowing in from the smog with...
Swiiish
Roberts
Those beatniks get on my nerves! I'll try French radio...
Roberts
She loves you !!!

In Woodside House I made my first friend outside of school – Peter Bottrell – a guy from Australia. I learned English playing with Peter and our Action Men.*

*ACTION MAN, the British version of G.I. Joe, was released in 1966.

54

THIS REALM, THIS ENGLAND*

Rolls Royce «Silver Shadow», 1965

* Richard II, King Richard, II, 1.

At the French Lycée in London, in South Kensington, I didn't have much trouble fitting in, but I was the smallest in my class, and I often wished I didn't look so Asian.

CHING CHANG CHONG!

?!

If only I could be like him!

Care for some gum, Caroline?

I thought I was too scrawny. I didn't like my slanted eyes ---

I wanna be a muscle man!

And my hair is too Chinese!

I made bug-eyes in hopes of unslanting them.

I wanted a long, straight nose. I tried the clothespin method.

I hade my flad dostrils!

"Bodybuilding for Beginners"

I want to hab a node like Mama and Domi's!

SNOOZE

There were a lot of foreigners at the London Lycée, though most students were British. The children of French expatriates were in the minority. You could recognize them by their classic outfits. In general, the British were more with it.

All the boys were in love with the class beauty: Caroline C.

Every morning on the way to the Lycée, I would buy a war comic, the kind all British boys loved. In Great Britain, many people said they had known their finest hour during the Second World War.

I liked French, history, English, and art ---

Marcelino wrote a very nice essay: an old suit of armor tells the story of its past. With a lovely drawing!

I hope Caroline will be impressed!

Caroline dozing ---

SNOOZE

← My drawing

Tough luck, I was lousy at football! A bus would drive us to a far-off pitch in the southern suburbs, Raynes Park, a dismal place ---

♪♫ THE DIRTY GERMANS CROSSED THE RHINE! PAAARLEZ-VOO?

I'm gonna throw up!!

I hated those cold, damp afternoons on the football field. I always ended up playing goalie. I did the least damage there.

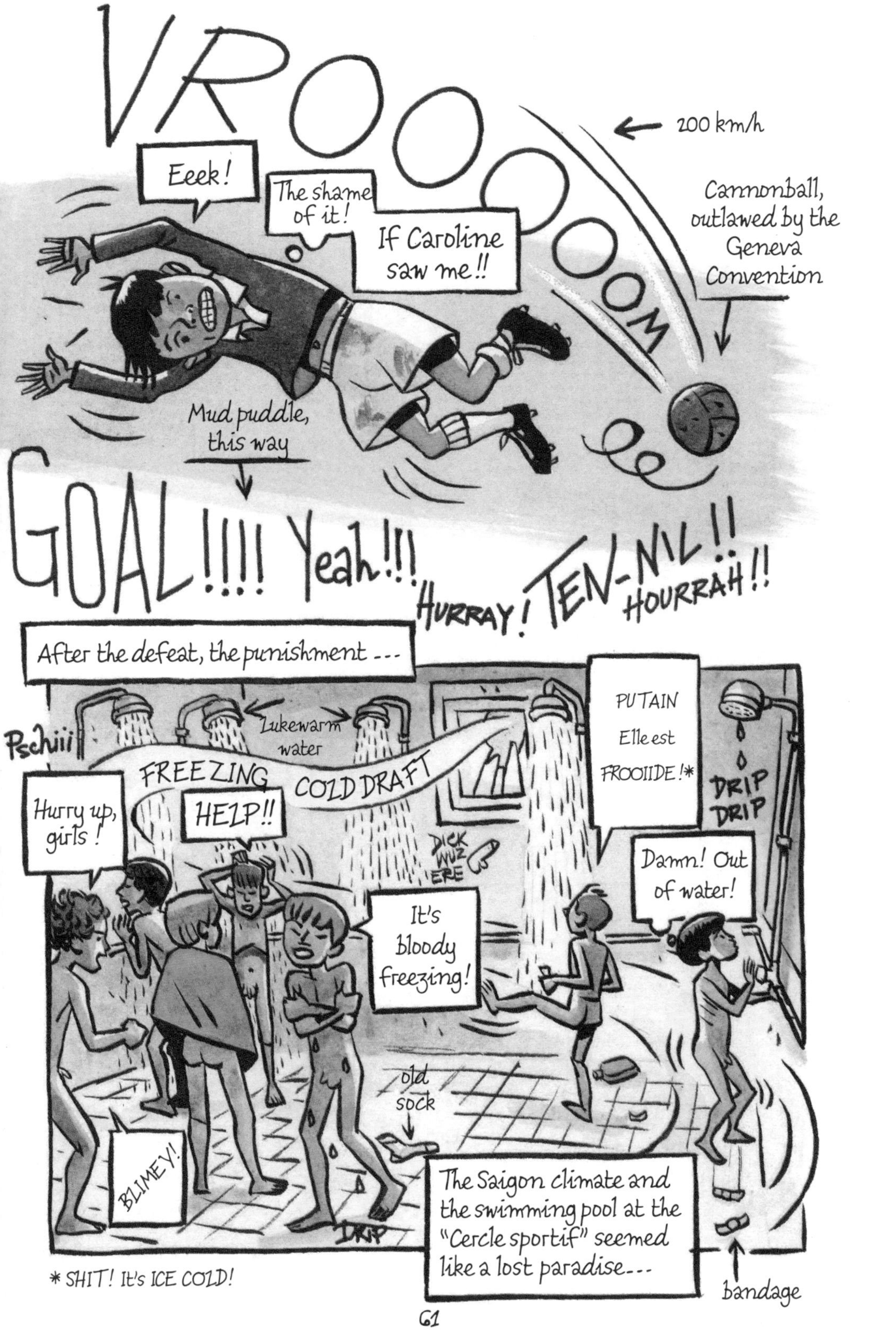
VROOOOOOOM
200 km/h
Eeek!
The shame of it!
If Caroline saw me!!
Cannonball, outlawed by the Geneva Convention
Mud puddle, this way
GOAL!!!! Yeah!!!
HURRAY! TEN-NIL!! HOURRAH!!
After the defeat, the punishment ...
Pschiii
Lukewarm water
FREEZING COLD DRAFT
PUTAIN Elle est FROOIIDE!*
DRIP DRIP
Hurry up, girls!
HELP!!
DICK WUZ ERE
Damn! Out of water!
It's bloody freezing!
old sock
BLIMEY!
DRIP
The Saigon climate and the swimming pool at the "Cercle sportif" seemed like a lost paradise...
bandage
* SHIT! It's ICE COLD!

But London in 1965 wasn't all fog and rain. A new wave was starting to shake up Olde Englande. You could see it in the clothes.

You could hear it in the air --- London was starting to swing.

* "Louie Louie", The Kingsmen, 1963.

My parents were looking for a small house to buy. After all sorts of adventures, they chose a townhouse located on a cul-de-sac on Wimbledon Hill. At the end of 1965, we moved into 6C Grosvenor Hill Road.

TIGER VS. ELEPHANT

* "The pleasure of love lasts but a while---" From the ballad "Plaisir d'amour" by Jean-Pierre Claris de Florian, 1784

*Pronounced "Teen" (Tin's nickname was Tintin).

I wonder how things are going in Saigon.

You'll give me the stamp for my collection?

Oh, no! Listen to this!

Sài Gòn, 21 July, 1965

Dear Marco,
You know the floating restorant Mây Cảnh on the Sài Gòn River where we ate chao tôm shrimps on sugar cane sticks (yum!) with my parents? Two bombs went off there last week!

GASP!

SHIIIIT!

Horrible! There were 40 ~~kelld~~ killed and many wounded. Papa says the VC uzed Claymore mines that shoot steel balls everywhere!!

In 1965, in response to the massive build-up of GIs in Vietnam, the NLF carried out a series of attacks. One of the most *deadly* was at the MY CANH Restaurant.

The attack on the floating restaurant was carefully orchestrated by a top-secret NLF unit, the F-100 group, made up of explosive specialists trained in a Viêt-Cong hideout – the tunnels of Cu Chi – some 40 kilometers from Saigon. For days, the head of the F-100 group, Nguyên Van Sâm, scouted the location ---

Hmm --- Weekends are the busiest time ---

Nguyễn Văn Sâm

On the appointed day, pretending to be an ordinary citizen, Sâm parked his motorbike on the wharf in front of the restaurant, and walked away. Later, an associate set his bicycle next to the scooter. In the saddlebags were two Claymore mines pointed toward the target.

OK, I'll leave my bike next to Sâm's scooter and get out of here!

2nd mine

1st mine

peepsight

The Claymore was an American directional fragmentation antipersonnel mine that shot hundreds of ball bearings in a 60-degree arc in front of the device.

FRONT TOWARD ENEMY

folding legs

detonator well

The triggering device was a rigged wristwatch whose second and hour hand had been removed. A battery wire was inserted through a hole drilled in the face. When the minute hand, set to the decided delay time, reached that wire, completing the circuit, the mine EXPLODED!

Tic Tic
Tic Tic

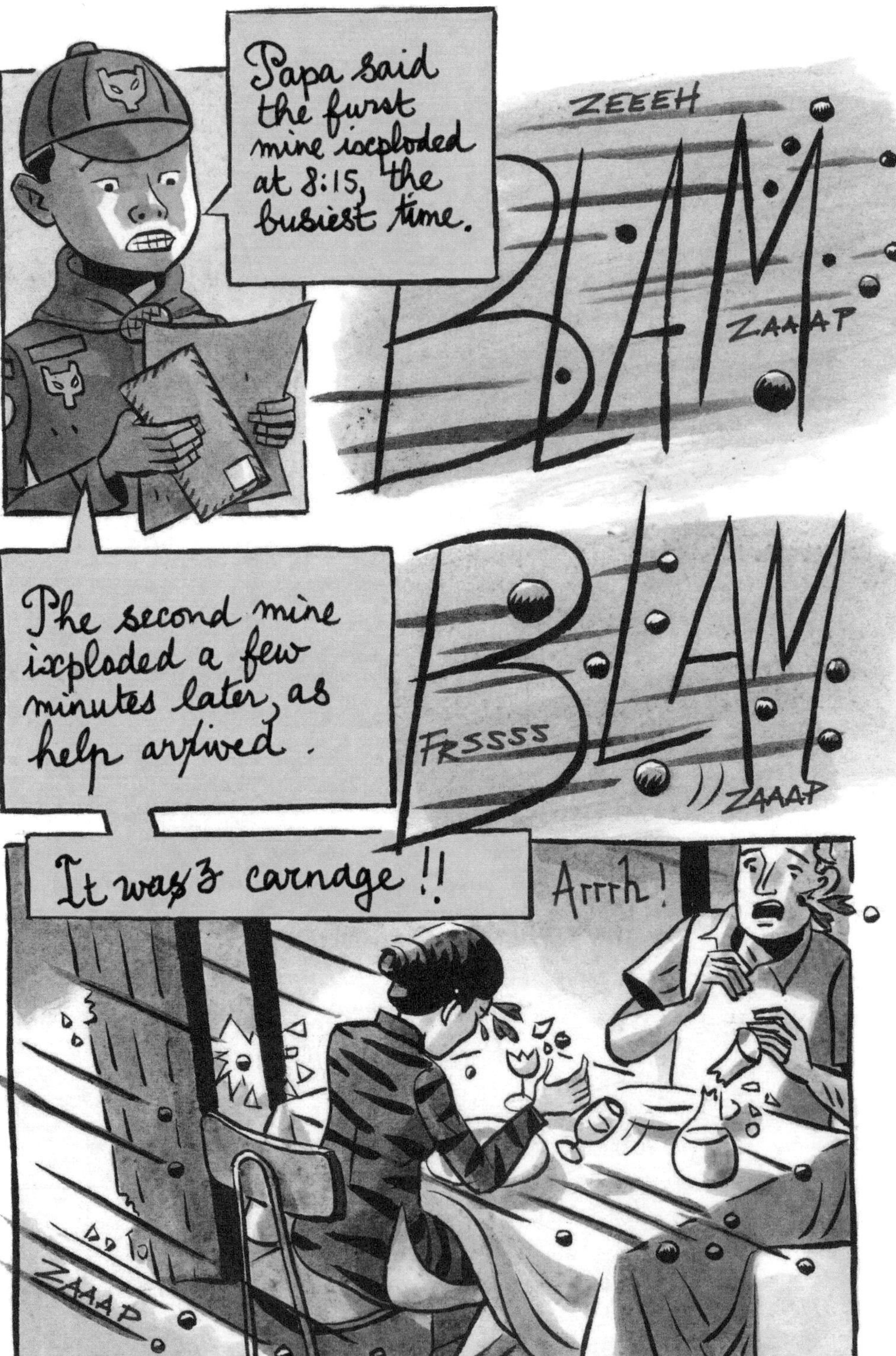
Papa said the furst mine icxploded at 8:15, the busiest time.
ZEEEH
BLAM
ZAAAP
The second mine icxploded a few minutes later, as help arfived.
BLAM
FRSSSS
ZAAAP
It was 3 carnage!!
Arrrh!
ZAAAP

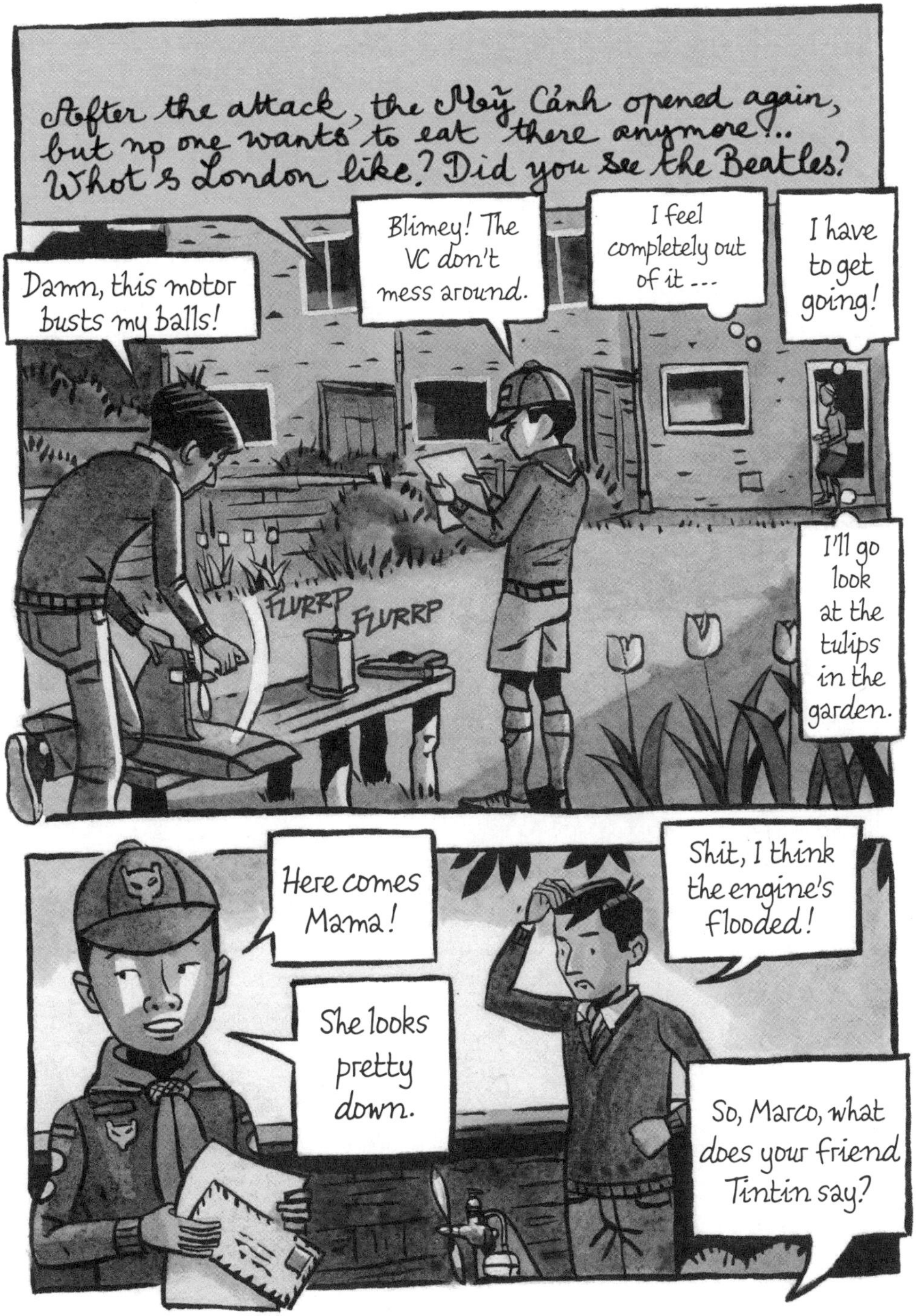
After the attack, the Mỹ Cảnh opened again, but no one wants to eat there anymore!.. What's London like? Did you see the Beatles?
Damn, this motor busts my balls!
Blimey! The VC don't mess around.
I feel completely out of it ...
I have to get going!
FLURRP
FLURRP
I'll go look at the tulips in the garden.
Here comes Mama!
She looks pretty down.
Shit, I think the engine's flooded!
So, Marco, what does your friend Tintin say?

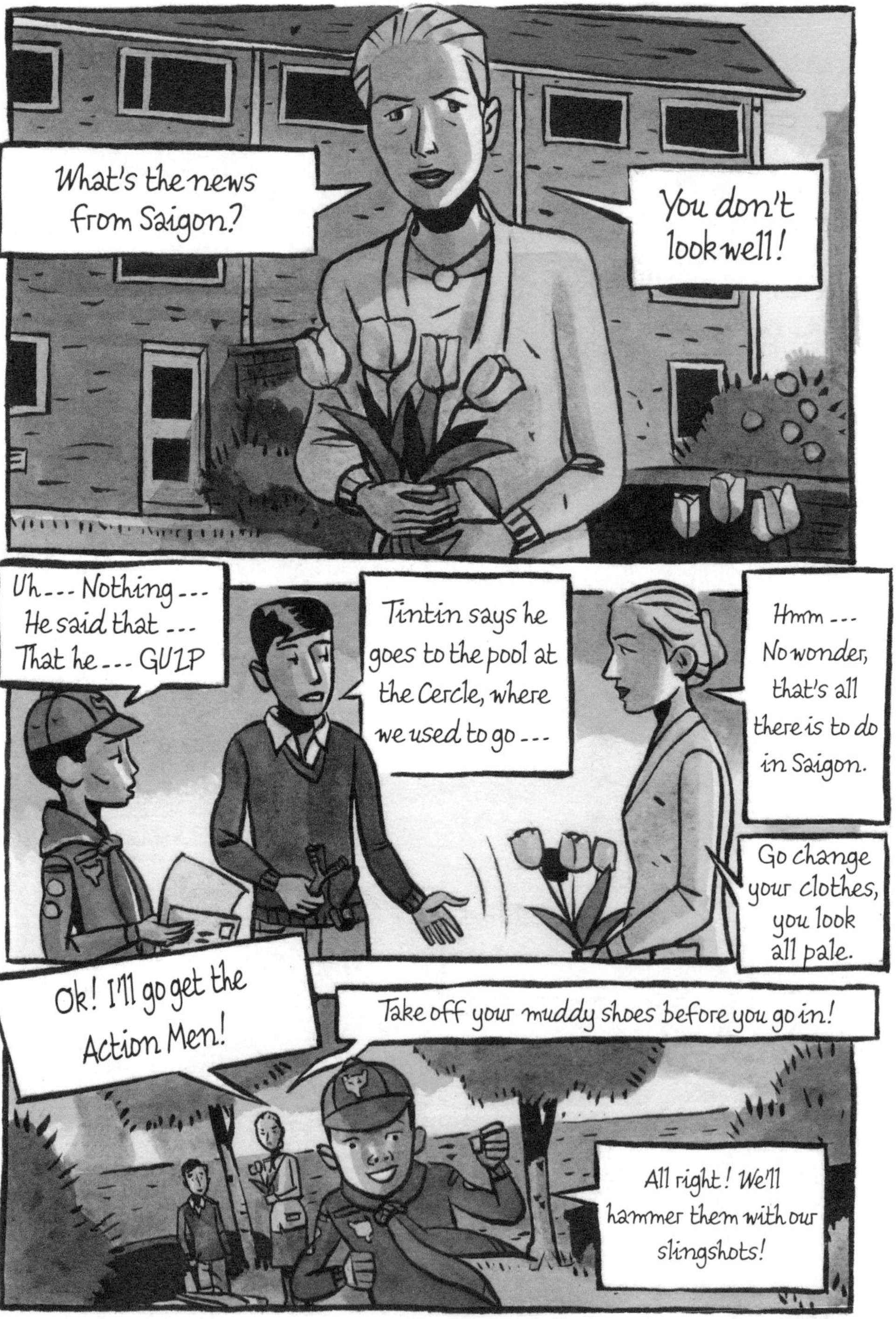
What's the news from Saigon?
You don't look well!
Uh--- Nothing--- He said that--- That he--- GULP
Tintin says he goes to the pool at the Cercle, where we used to go---
Hmm--- No wonder, that's all there is to do in Saigon.
Go change your clothes, you look all pale.
Ok! I'll go get the Action Men!
Take off your muddy shoes before you go in!
All right! We'll hammer them with our slingshots!

SUBURBAN HOUSEWIFE BLUES

Our townhouse, rather modest compared to others, sat at the top of a hill, off the "village" and backing onto the "Common." The hill looked down on the station with its "high street" lined with shops and a lower middle-class district.

"Sexy" 6C Grosvenor Hill Road

In 6A lived a retired officer, the "Major." His wife put herself in charge of relations with the neighbors.

Children must be restrained!

- - -

In 6B, Mrs. Miles looked like the Queen of England as she tended her roses.

Mrs Trong (sic), could you ask your sons not to bombard my rose bushes with their football?

In 6D, the Dallys. He was a former officer of the Royal Navy who became a solicitor. His wife – Phillida, by name! – was a hyperactive housewife ---

Fancy another Marmite sandwich, Marco?

Uhh--- Yes please!

--- who had two really nice boys, David and Jonathan.

Mrs Trunog (sic), could Marco and Noëlle come out and play cricket with us?

In 6E, Mr. and Mrs. Brown, a hip young couple. He worked in advertising, designing Pirelli tire calendars, pneumatic pin-ups with big busts.

Miss July! Mmmm! WOW!!

In the autumn, my favorite holiday was GUY FAWKES NIGHT, November 5th. We got to play with explosives! The fireworks commemorated the day in 1605 when a Catholic plot to blow up the very Protestant House of Lords was foiled.

The fireworks always put Mama on edge.

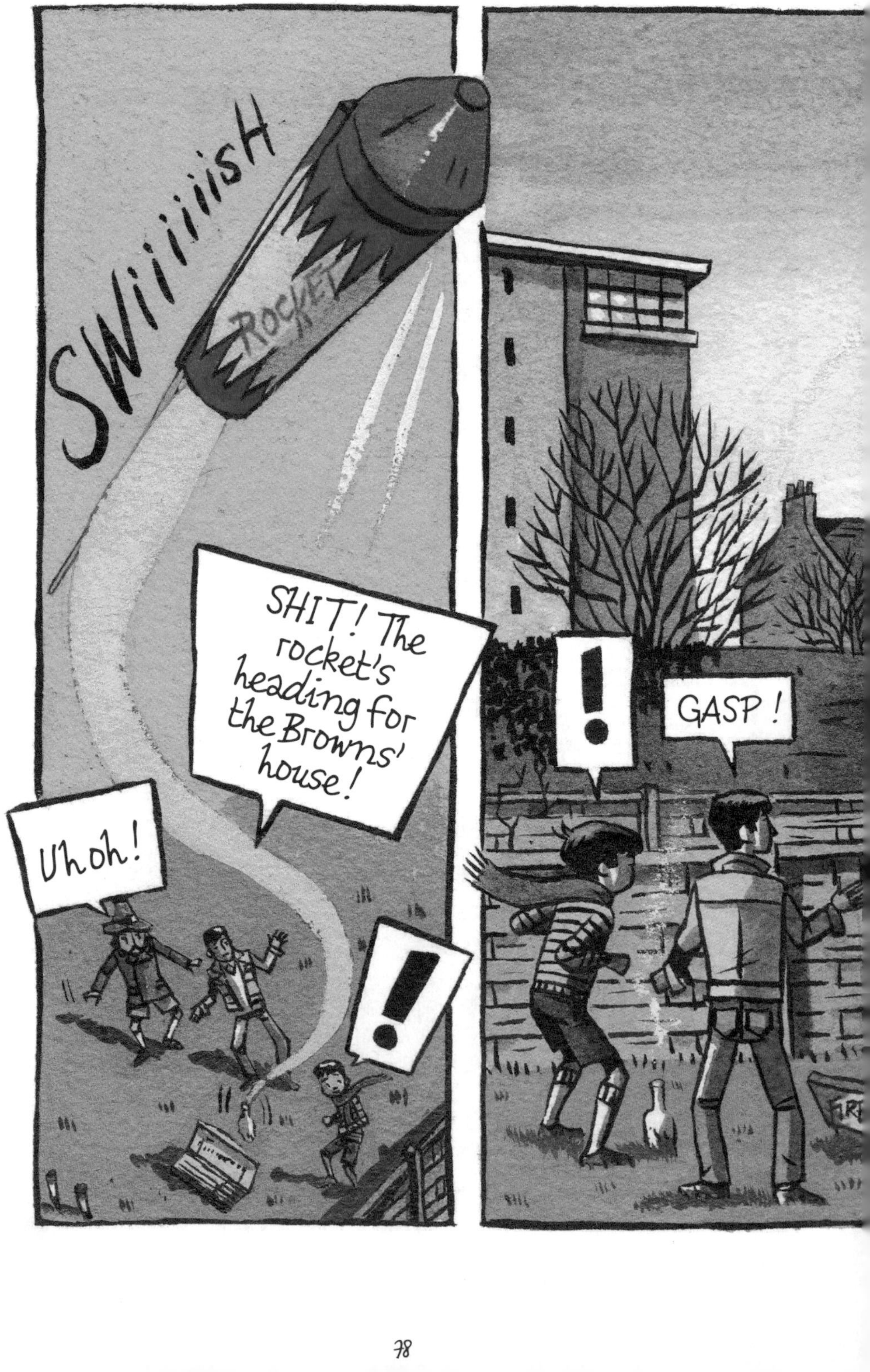
SWiiiiiisH
ROCKET
SHIT! The rocket's heading for the Browns' house!
Uh oh!
!
!
GASP !

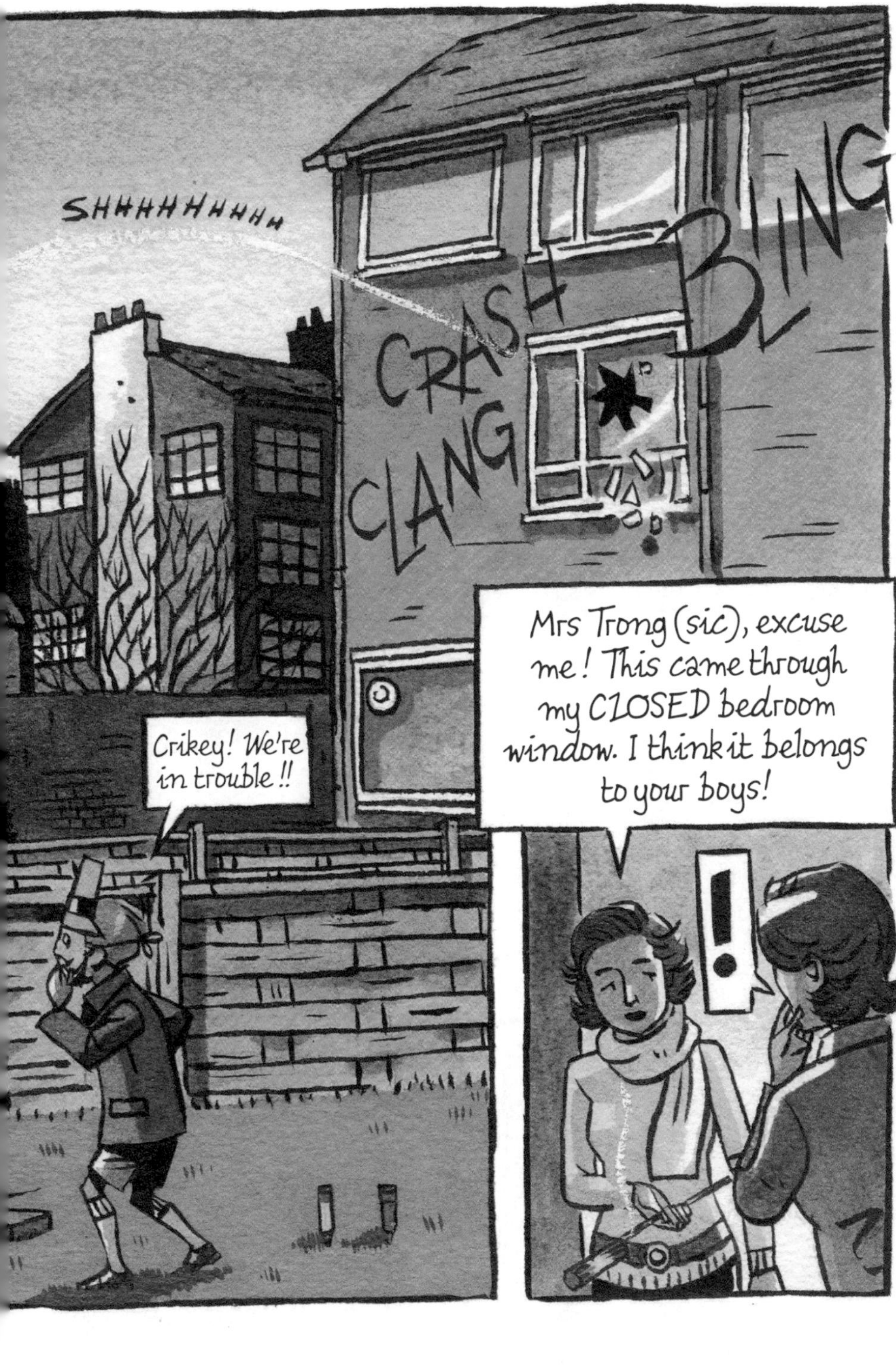
SHHHHHHHHH
CRASH
CLANG
BLING
Crikey! We're in trouble!!
Mrs Trong (sic), excuse me! This came through my CLOSED bedroom window. I think it belongs to your boys!
!

After her experience in Vietnam, Mama started to think that life as a suburban housewife was dull as dust ...

Now what's that racket?!

Turn down the news, I'm sick of it!

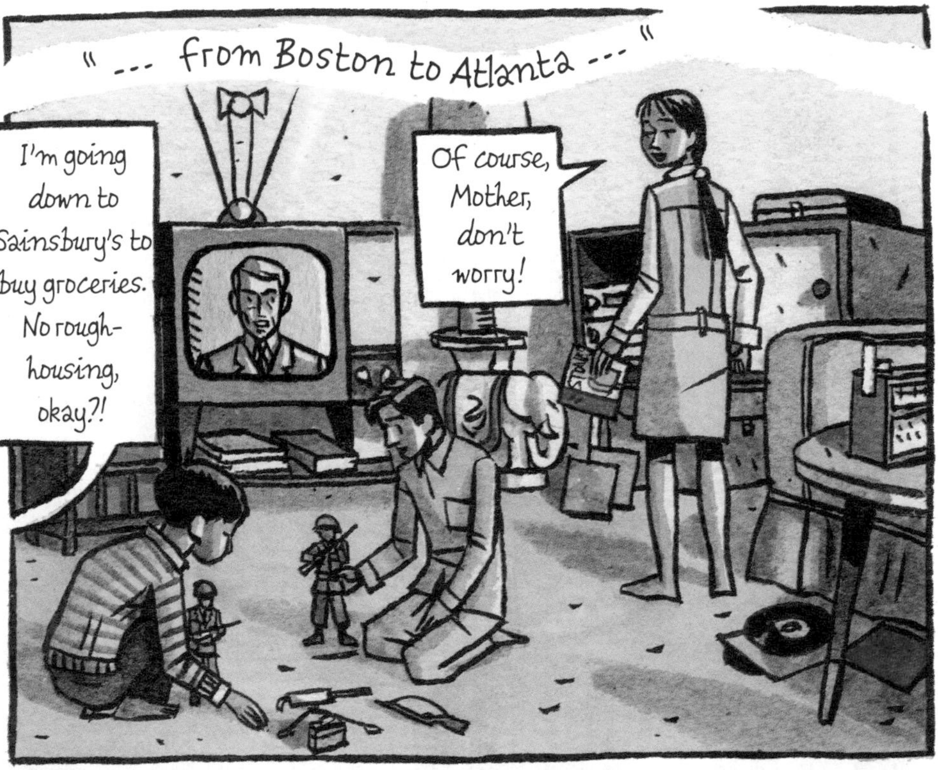
" --- from Boston to Atlanta --- "
I'm going down to Sainsbury's to buy groceries. No rough-housing, okay?!
Of course, Mother, don't worry!

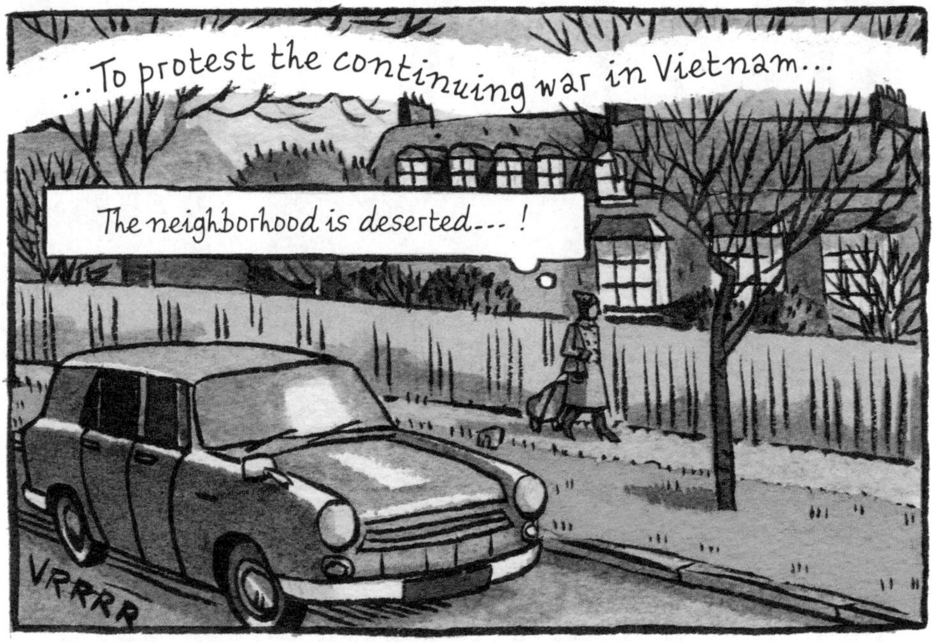
...To protest the continuing war in Vietnam...
The neighborhood is deserted--- !
VRRRR

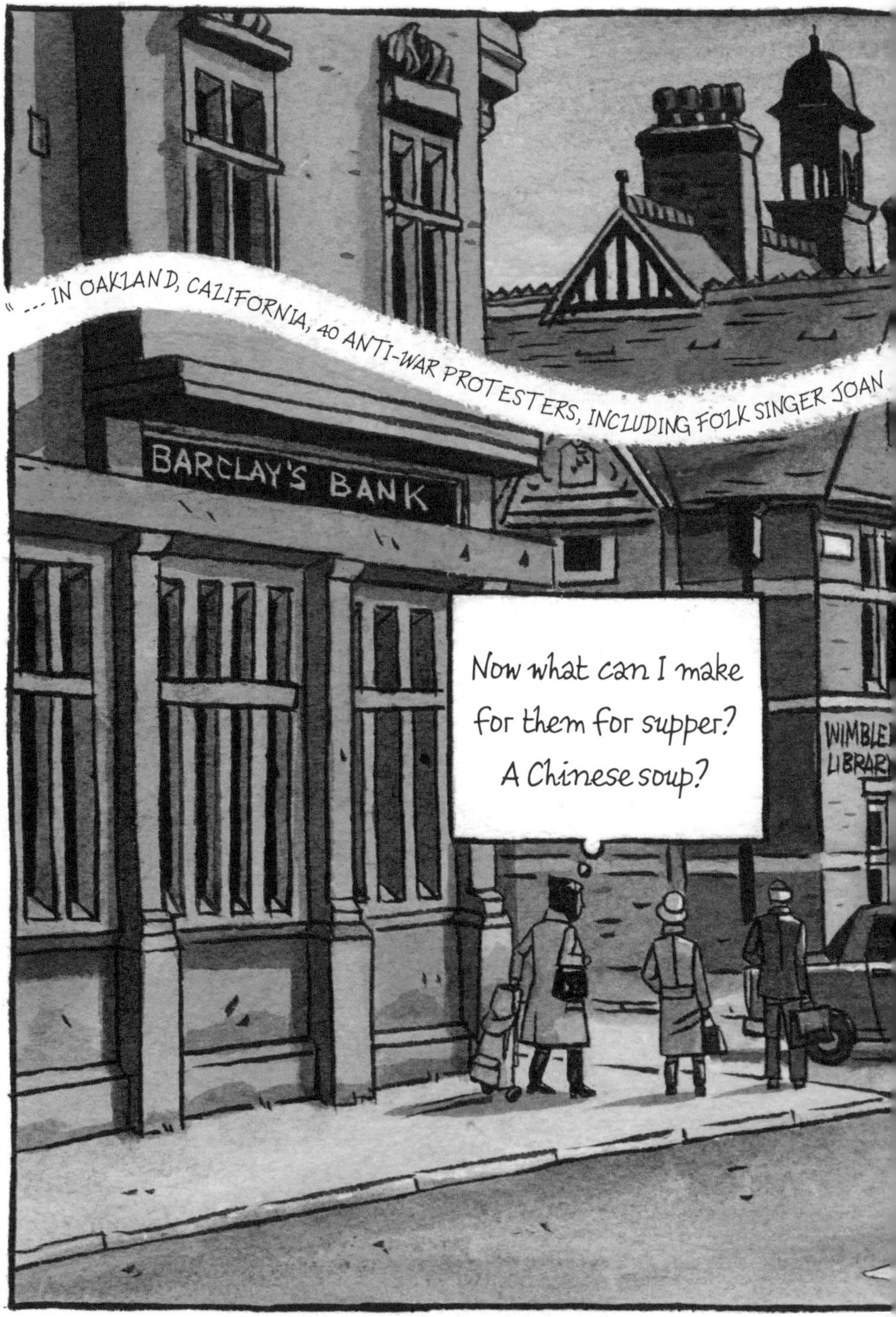
"... IN OAKLAND, CALIFORNIA, 40 ANTI-WAR PROTESTERS, INCLUDING FOLK SINGER JOAN
BARCLAY'S BANK
Now what can I make for them for supper? A Chinese soup?
WIMBLE
LIBRAR

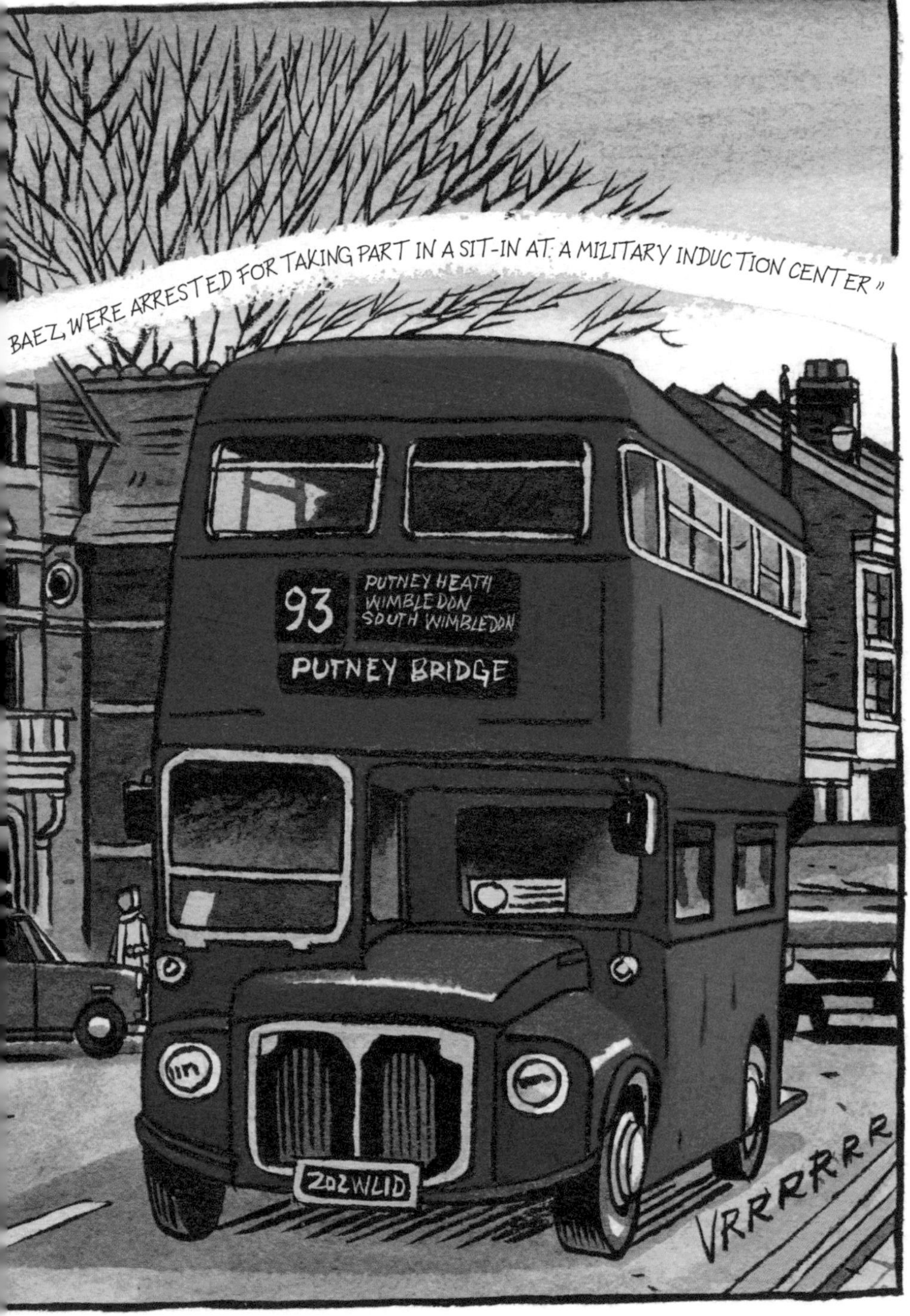
BAEZ, WERE ARRESTED FOR TAKING PART IN A SIT-IN AT A MILITARY INDUCTION CENTER"
93
PUTNEY HEATH
WIMBLEDON
SOUTH WIMBLEDON
PUTNEY BRIDGE
202 WLID
VRRRRRR

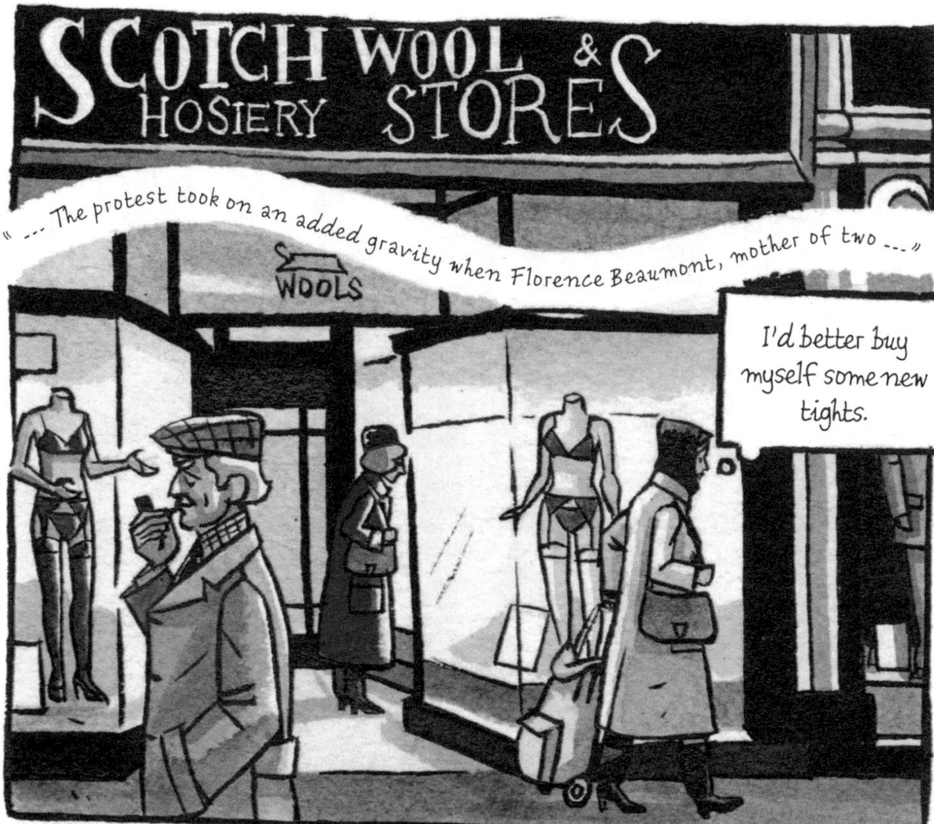
SCOTCH WOOL & HOSIERY STORES
"... The protest took on an added gravity when Florence Beaumont, mother of two ..."
WOOLS
I'd better buy myself some new tights.

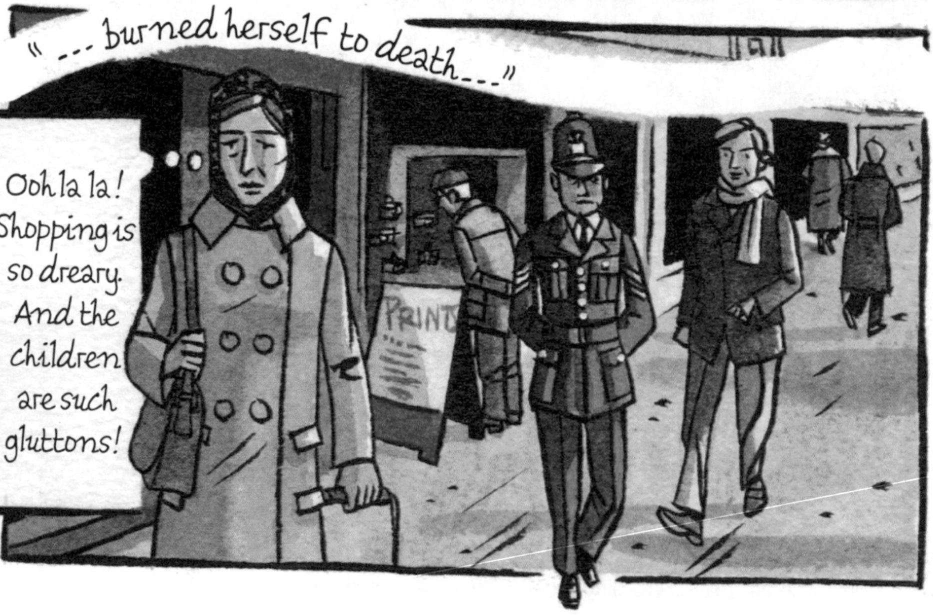
"... burned herself to death..."
Ooh la la! Shopping is so dreary. And the children are such gluttons!

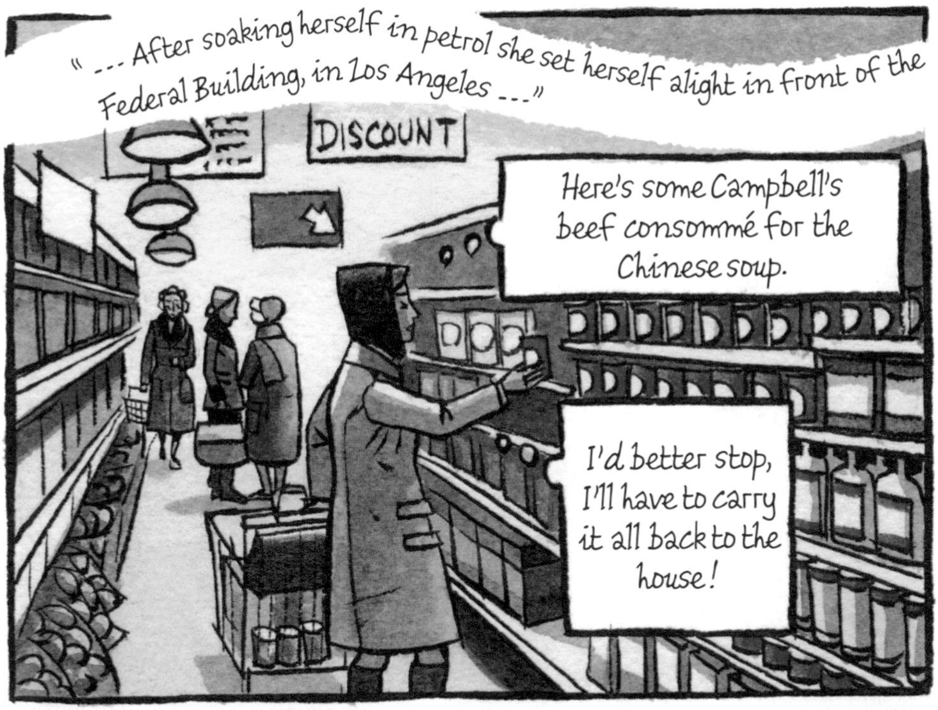
"... After soaking herself in petrol she set herself alight in front of the Federal Building, in Los Angeles ..."
DISCOUNT
Here's some Campbell's beef consommé for the Chinese soup.
I'd better stop, I'll have to carry it all back to the house!

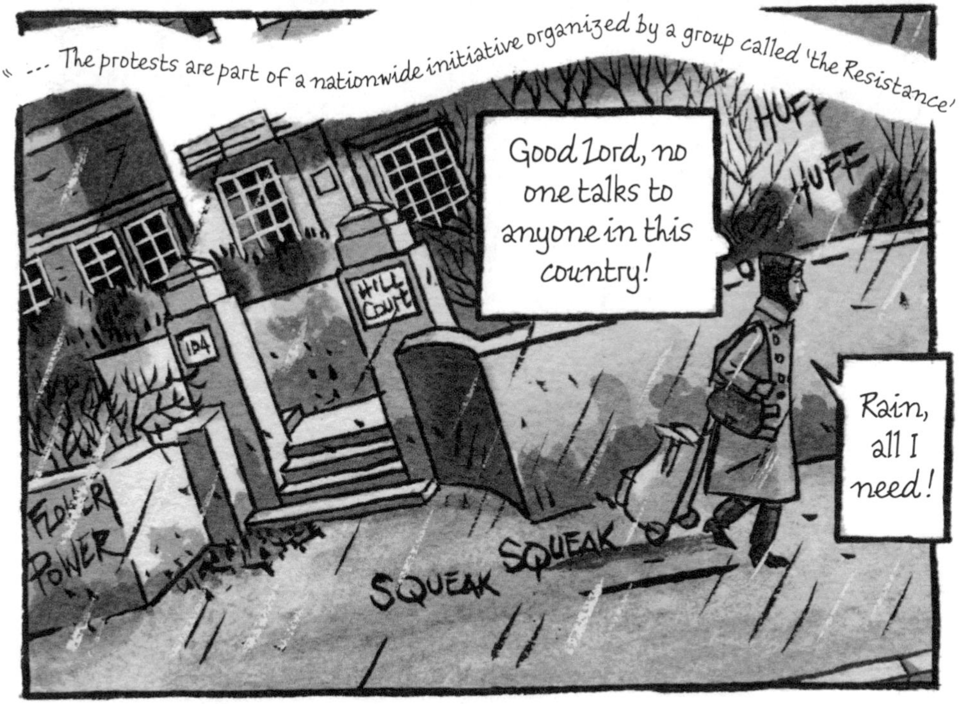
"... The protests are part of a nationwide initiative organized by a group called 'the Resistance'
HUFF
HUFF
Good Lord, no one talks to anyone in this country!
HILL COURT
104
Rain, all I need!
FLOWER POWER
SQUEAK
SQUEAK

SQUEAK
SQUEAK

* Diazepam was marketed in 1963 under the name Valium.

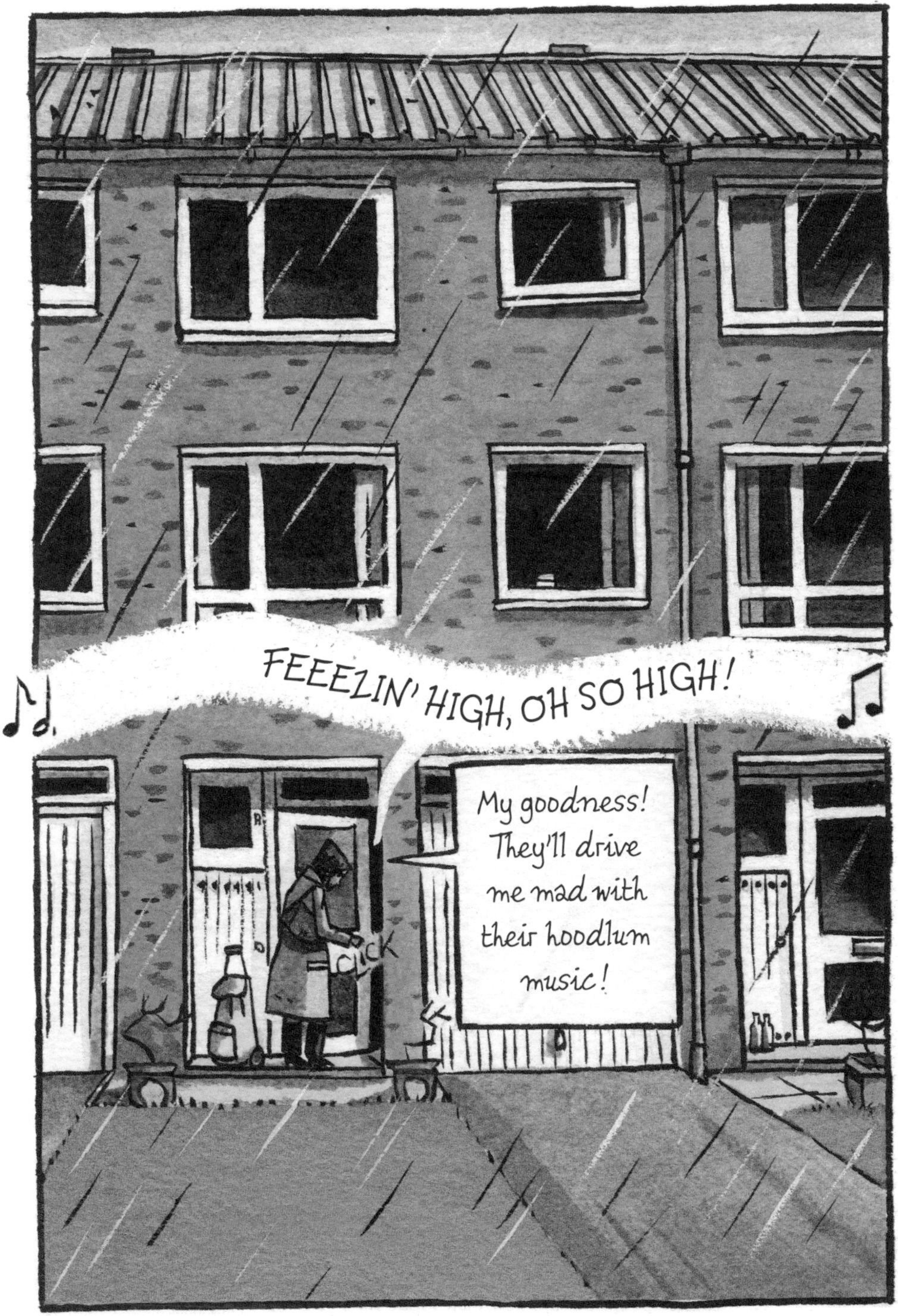
FEEELIN' HIGH, OH SO HIGH!
My goodness! They'll drive me mad with their hoodlum music!
CLICK

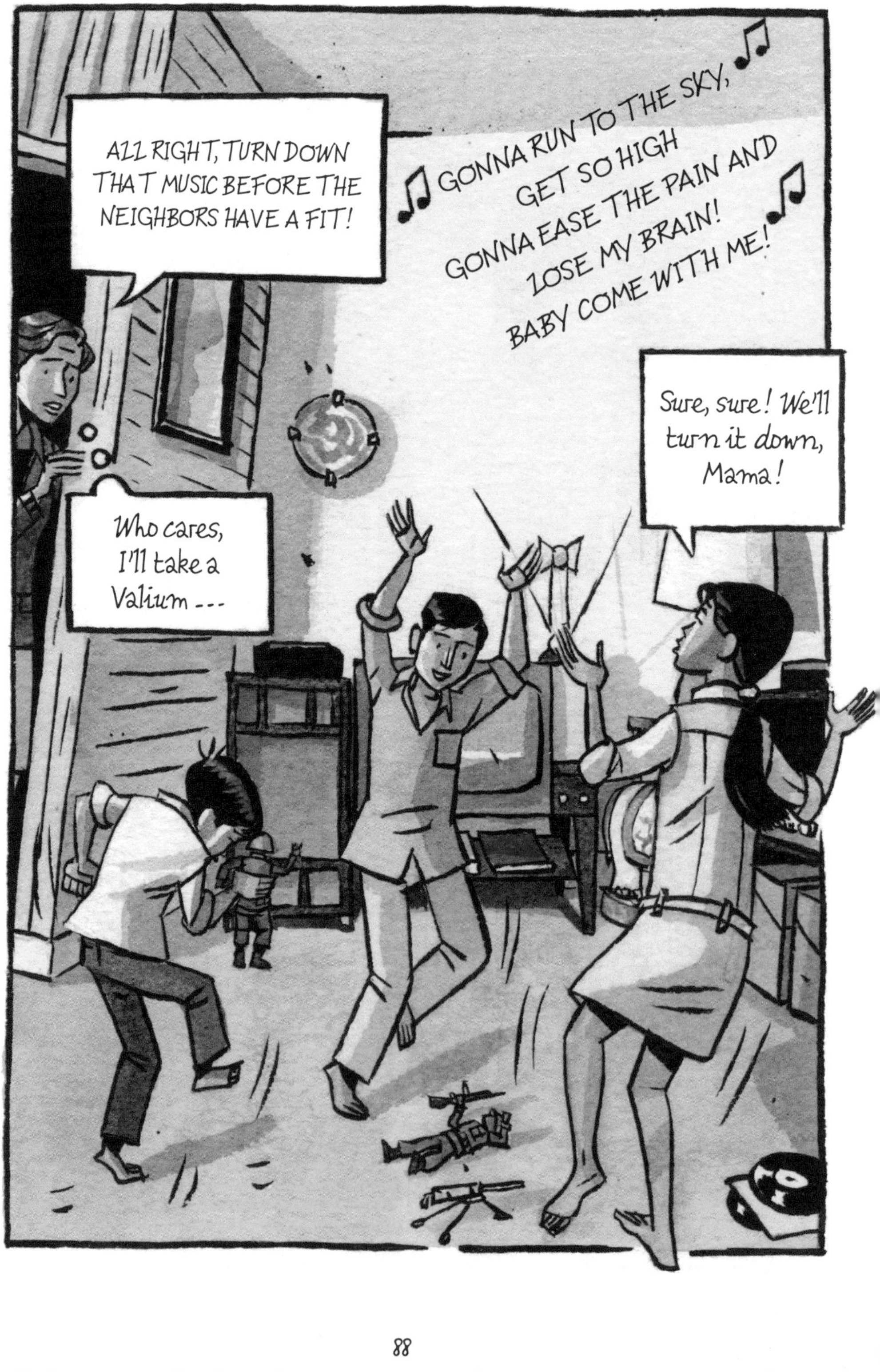
ALL RIGHT, TURN DOWN THAT MUSIC BEFORE THE NEIGHBORS HAVE A FIT!
GONNA RUN TO THE SKY, GET SO HIGH GONNA EASE THE PAIN AND LOSE MY BRAIN! BABY COME WITH ME!
Who cares, I'll take a Valium ...
Sure, sure! We'll turn it down, Mama!

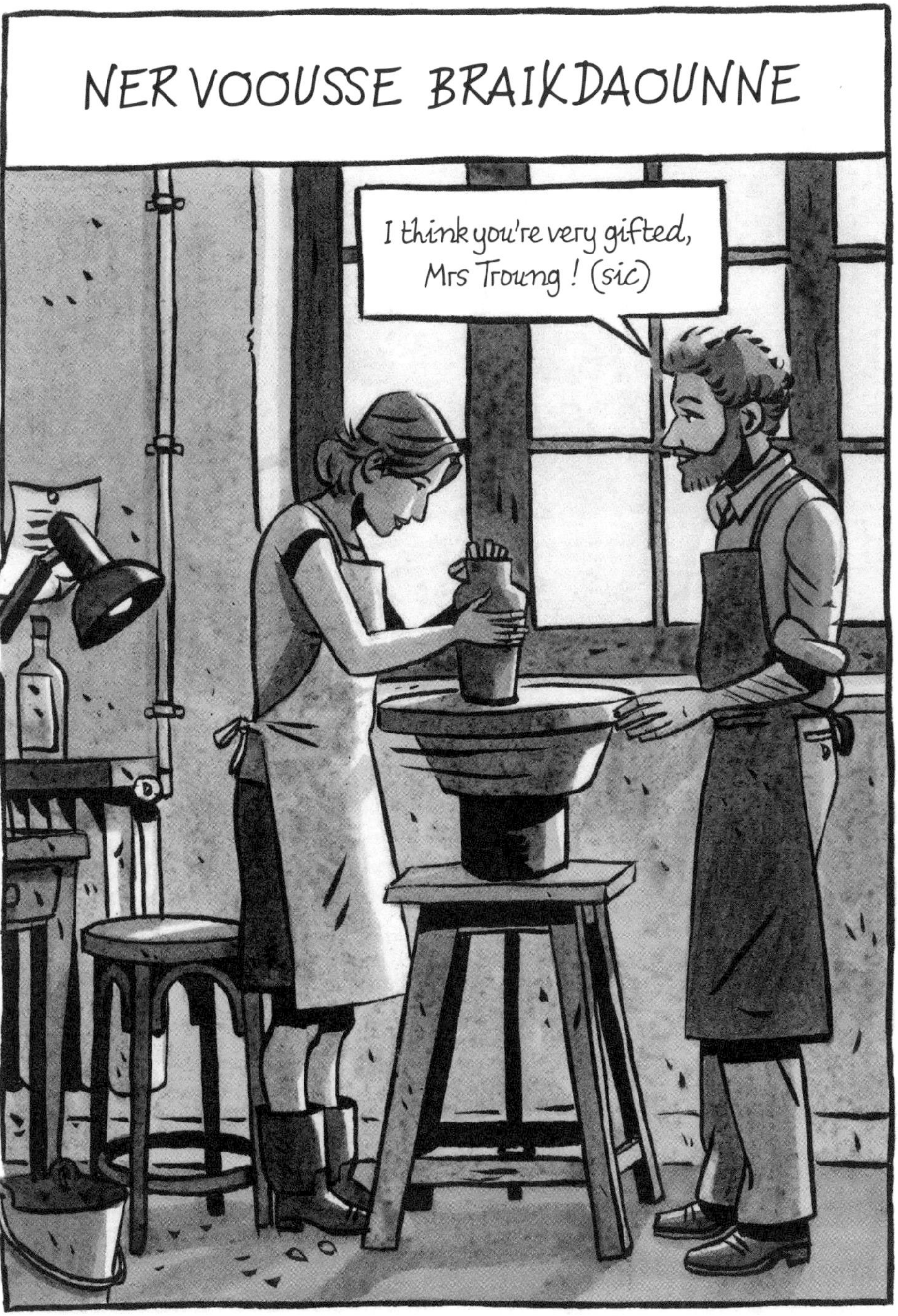
NERVOOUSSE BRAIKDAOUNNE
I think you're very gifted, Mrs Troung ! (sic)

Mama considered her life a long list of chores.

Now, what should we eat tonight? I could make hash out of the leftovers ---

Later ---

Mamaaaa!

Noëlle is waking up! She had a nasty fever this morning.

101.5 !!

Just my luck! I won't be able to go to the pottery show!

Normally, Mama *didn't* miss a single class with a fashionable potter whose studio was near Wimbledon.

Yvette, I want to exhibit your works along with those of my best students at the Merton Arts ___ and Craft show next month!

Oh, Tony, I ham veeree deeliited!

← BLUSH

But Noëlle's fever kept Mama from participating in the Merton group show ---

My husband is too tired after work, and he can never help out.

I'm just a servant, always scrubbing and scraping!

Are you crying, Mama?

Oh, it doesn't matter!

Language was another obstacle. One day, Mama went looking for the building supervisor.

Excuuuse mee, ouaire izz zee underteker pleez?

My name is BOND...

James Bond gun

I'm sorry?! The undertaker?!

Has someone passed away?!

Surely, you must mean the "caretaker"?

TWEET TWEET!

Av you beurd shits pleez?

?!

Hee hee!

We had a canary named Tweet. We covered the bottom of his cage with disposable sheets of sandpaper.

Mama, you have to say "biiird sheeets."

I said "beurd shits."

That's what birds drop on your head, Mama!

Mama felt isolated. She had the suburban blues.

It's terrible, the shops close at 5:30!!

And it rains all the time!!

Look! Dinky Toys put out a Batmobile!

CULLEN'S

I want one!

Zeh Brrreeteesh ouehzeere!!*

Not a sound from the neighbors!

Wimbledon is deadly!

It's impossible to make friends!

I hope Mama will let us watch TOP OF THE POPS.

You bet! She really bugs me when she gets started!

* "The British weather!!"

Her recriminations, often audible, sometimes foretold more violent storms that almost always broke out *during the forced confinement of the long British weekends.*

Papa often ended up the main target of Mama's anger. He would suffer through a bombardment of blame.

At times like that, a 1966 Rolling Stones hit echoed unhappily in our heads.

Their arguments could go on for hours ---

Up until then, the action was limited to screaming matches. Mama did have a difficult life. But when the switch was thrown, the madness would begin.

* "Potty": British slang for "crazy."

Papa was out of ideas. He finally called in our family GP,
Dr. Wassell-Smith.

This shot will get you nicely sedated, Mrs Troung (sic)!

Your wife will need a lot of rest, Mr Troung (sic).

Mama would sleep for hours. Calm was restored. We all felt relieved. And we all pitched in.

Papa, I'll make onion soup!

And we'll grate the cheese!

When she awoke, Mama seemed to be herself again ---

You kids are my guardian angels!

Maman!

We made you rice soup, Mama!

I'll put on the French radio!

Zouiiit

And life went back to normal ---

Bye, Mama! Don't do too much, okay?

Of course! Study hard at the Lycée, Mireille!

But the bad times kept returning. When things were calm, we hardly talked about the origins or possible causes of Mama's illness. One day, I'm not sure when, Papa told us some stories from the past.

Your mother's disorder began when Marco was born, in 1957 in Manila ---

After his birth, she had a terrible bout of madness. The doctors thought she'd lost her mind. She spent a month in a psychiatric hospital.

She was given electro-shocks ---

I was very afraid for her --- And for us ---

She came back, apparently cured, but she's been fragile ever since ---

Today, we'd say that Mama had post-partum depression. But back then they thought she was crazy ---

100

RAISING HELL

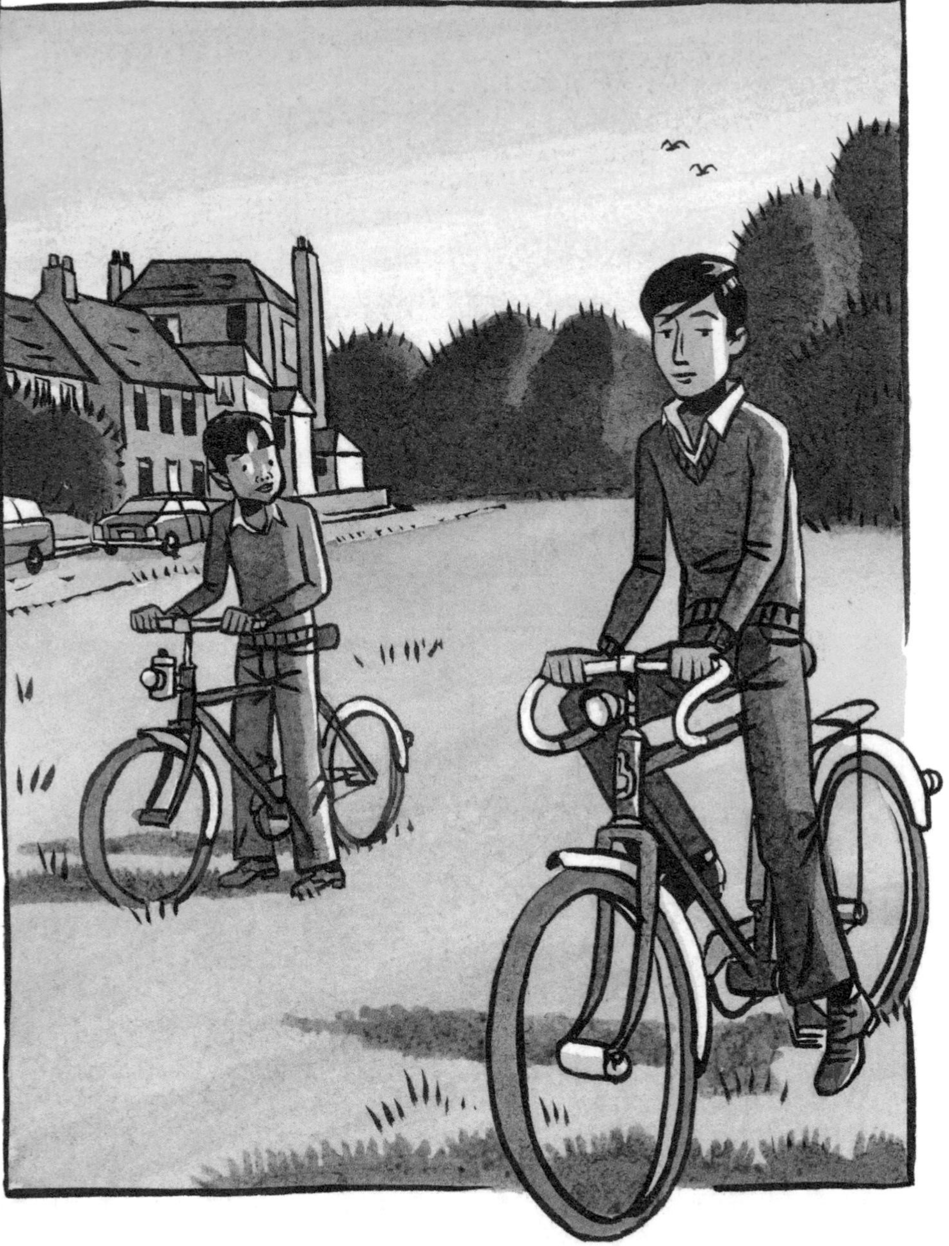

Summer vacations were a horror show for Mama. She dreaded having to take care of the teenagers we had turned into.

Boys! Go do your mischief on the Common!!

And bring me back my radio!

I'm gonna knock off the Kraut manning the machine gun!

Action Men

Shit! Mama wants us to go to the Common!

TALKIN' 'BOUT MY FAVORITE STATION! RADIO ONE!

Dominique was 14 in 1967, and I was 9.

He pedals like he's on fire!

People try to put us down...

Films were one of our favorite pastimes.

* Mahdi: the Expected One, the Redeemer.

Before every film, the national anthem was belted out and we had to stand. In the balcony, you were allowed to smoke.

* "The last show": World War II.

Dominique was slowly turning into a "bad boy." If Papa knew, with his ideas about obedience ---

I am the Mahdi! The Expected One!

Let mountains and deserts tremble!

Let cities shudder!

Lawrence Olivier →

What a boring film!

What a drag! Papa said to go to the barbershop after the show.

Right! Shitty! Short back and sides, huh?

Later ---

"Short back and sides." I hate that ass-kissing teacher's pet look!

Me too! I'd like to have the Beatles look.

Mod

CONFECTIONERY

WALL'S

LYONS MAY ZOO

Yeah, you'll get your Viêt-Cong look instead!

Oh-so-square!

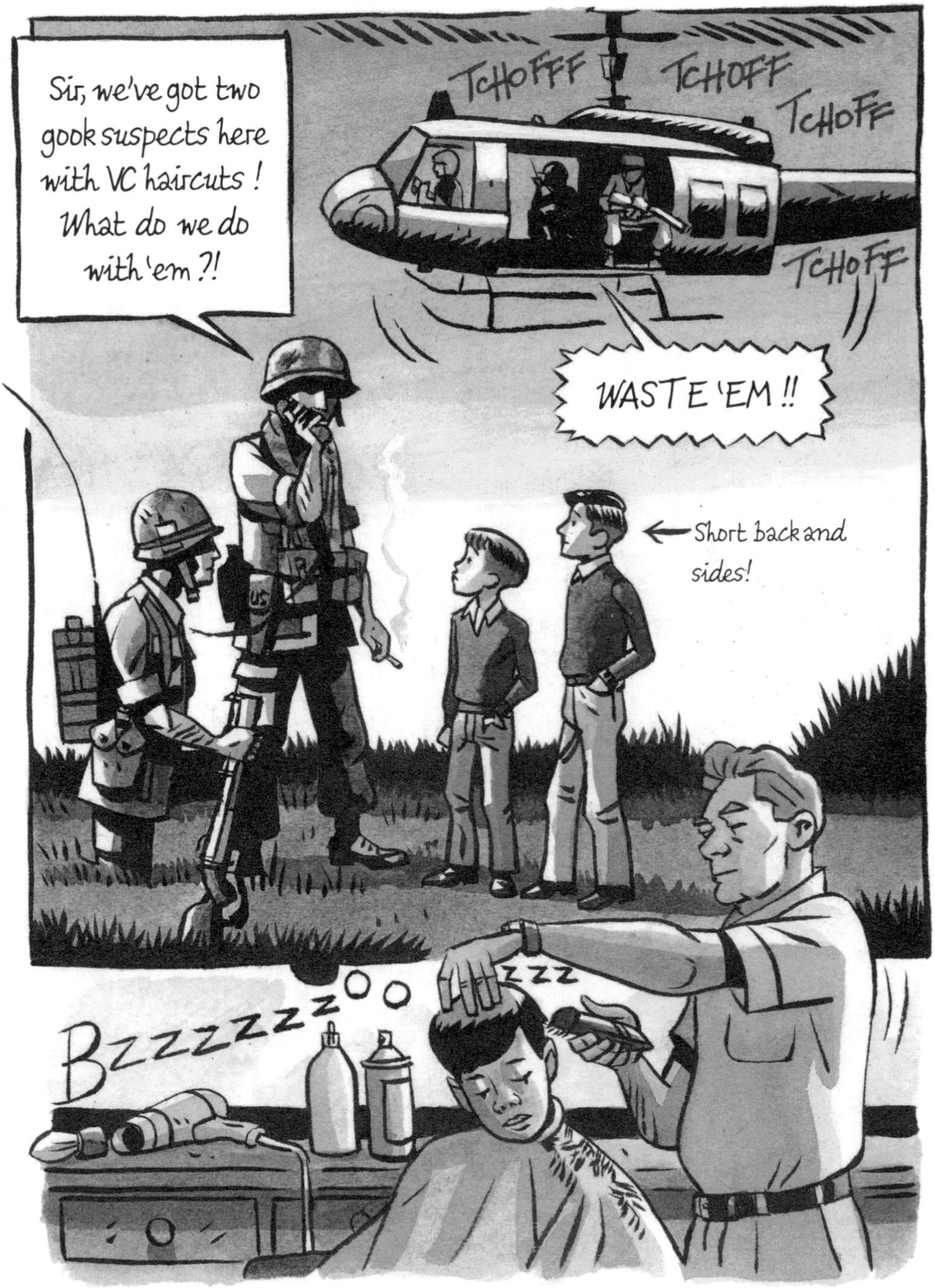
Sir, we've got two gook suspects here with VC haircuts ! What do we do with 'em ?!
TCHOFFF
TCHOFF
TCHOFF
TCHOFF
WASTE 'EM !!
Short back and sides!
BZZZZZZZ
ZZZ

Not too short, please!

Bzzzzzz

In Vietnam, they say when the GIs catch a peasant with a VC haircut, he could be tortured or killed!!

WOW! Look at those breasts!

Caroline's going to hate my short hair!

SNIFF! SNIFF!

Later...

We look pretty stupid with our VC look!

How come you always have your "Man from U.N.C.L.E." holster?!

I'm a spy from U.N.C.L.E.!!

More like a spy from UNCLE HO with your look! HA HA HA!

I saw you looking at the titty magazines at the barbershop!

YOU BUG ME!

Fold-up toy U.N.C.L.E. weapon

108

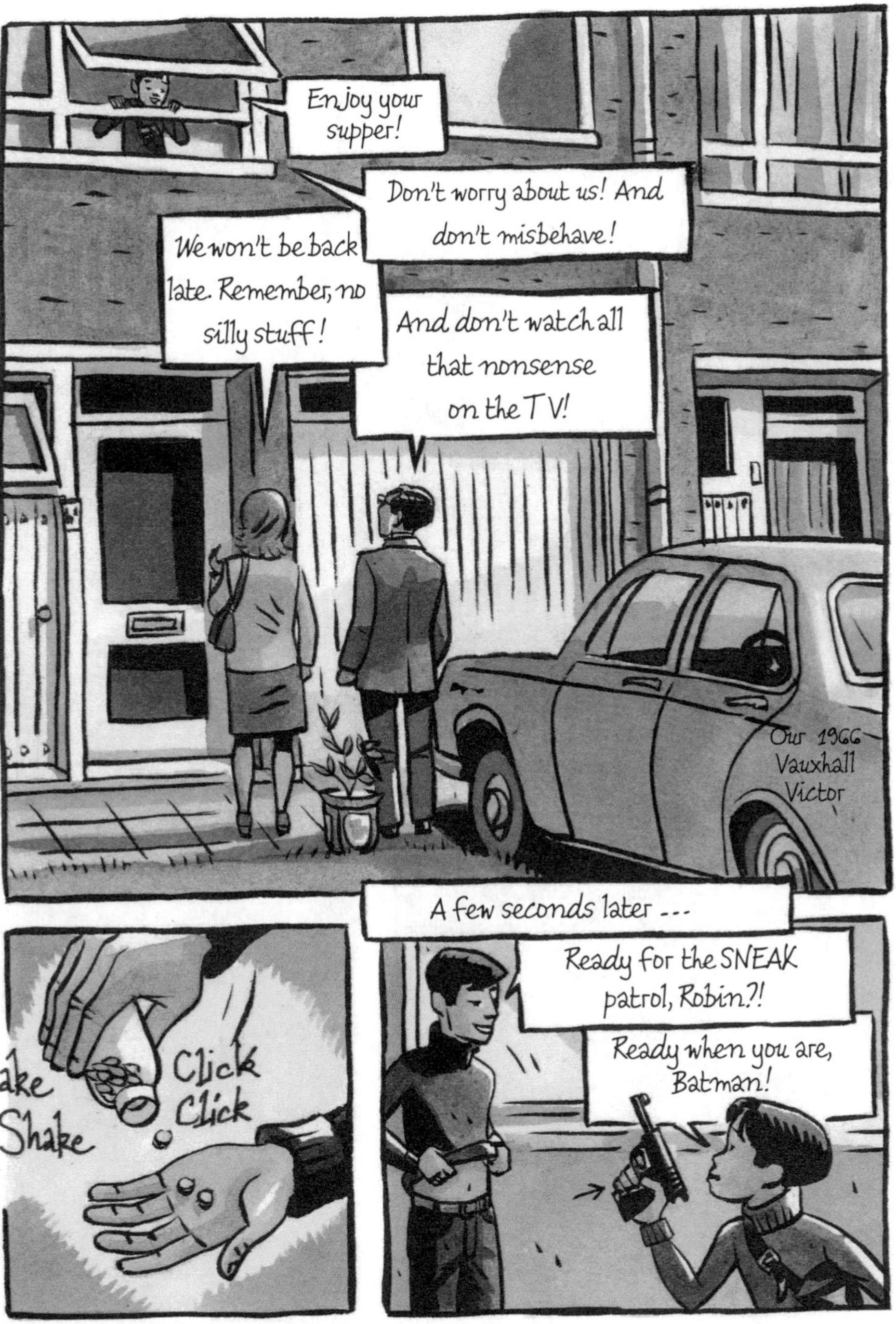
Enjoy your supper!
Don't worry about us! And don't misbehave!
We won't be back late. Remember, no silly stuff!
And don't watch all that nonsense on the TV!
Our 1966 Vauxhall Victor
A few seconds later ...
Shake Shake
Click Click
Ready for the SNEAK patrol, Robin?!
Ready when you are, Batman!

"Sneak" was one of our favorite words. It was the name of a game we invented in Saigon.

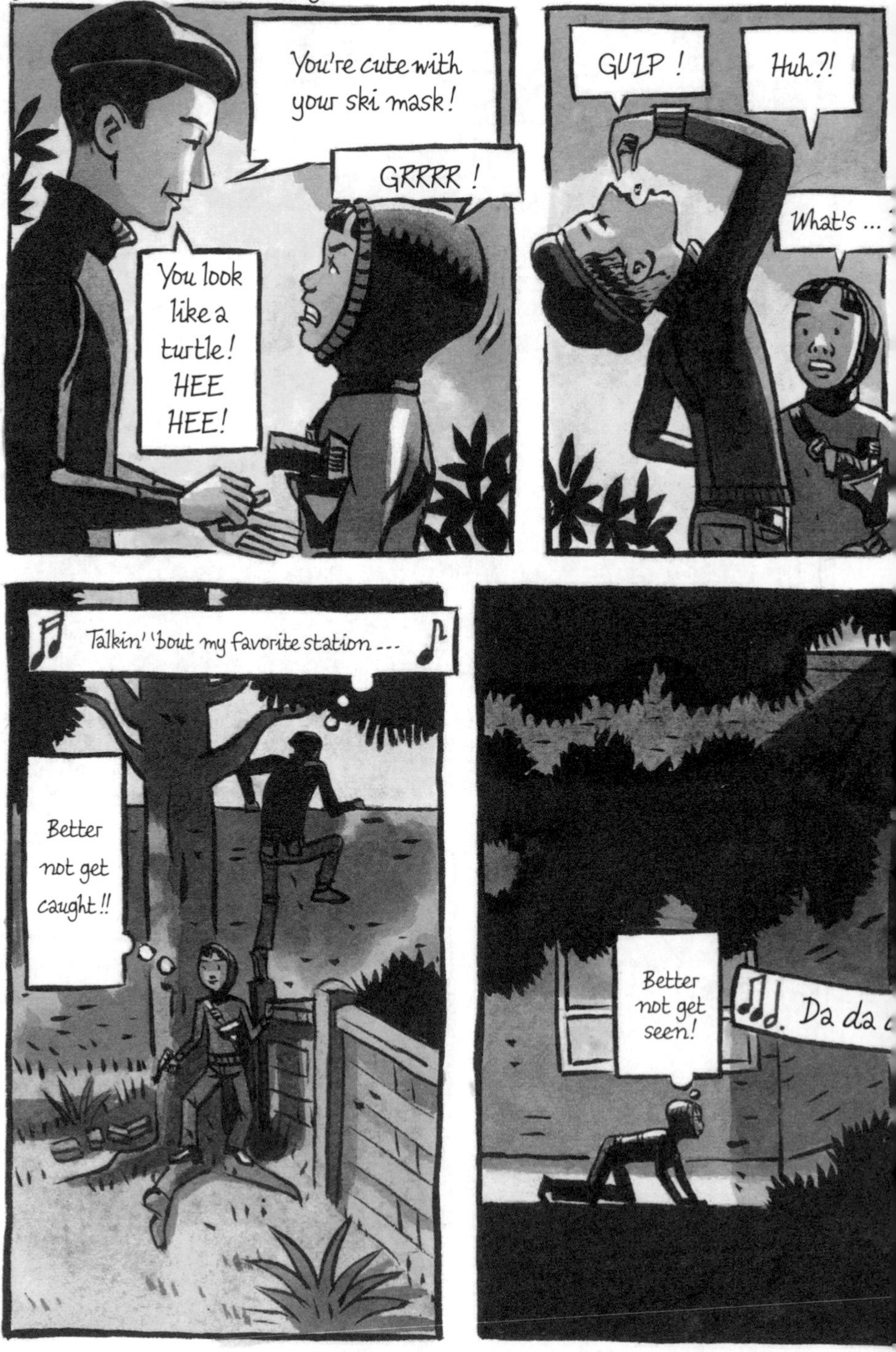
You're cute with your ski mask!
GRRRR!
You look like a turtle! HEE HEE!
GULP!
Huh?!
What's ...
Talkin' 'bout my favorite station ...
Better not get caught!!
Better not get seen!
Da da

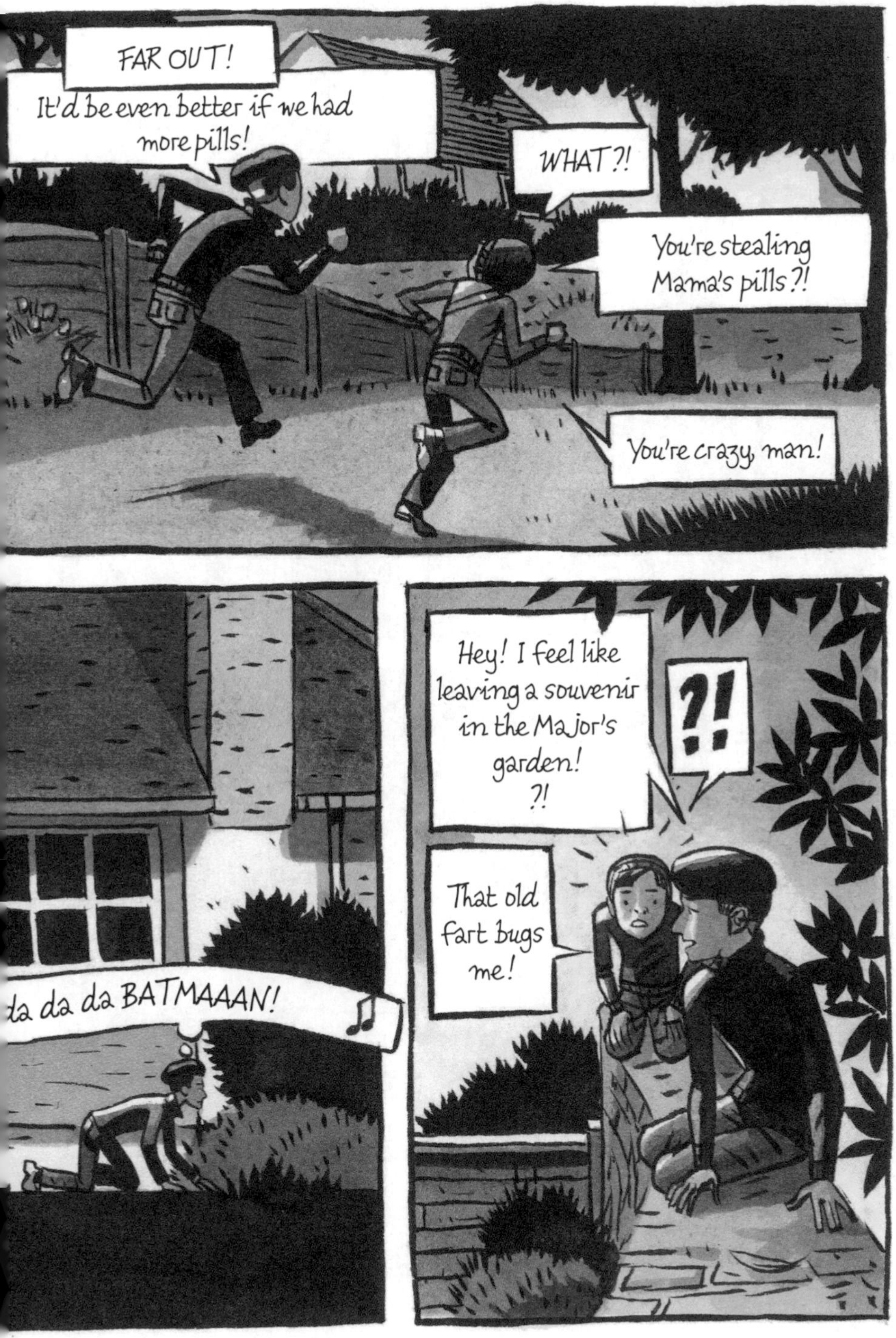
FAR OUT!
It'd be even better if we had more pills!
WHAT?!
You're stealing Mama's pills?!
You're crazy, man!
da da da BATMAAAN!
Hey! I feel like leaving a souvenir in the Major's garden!
?!
?!
That old fart bugs me!

*"Turn on, tune in, drop out" was a counterculture slogan coined by Timothy Leary.

PURPLE HAZE*

* In 1961-62, Jimi Hendrix was a paratrooper with the American 101st Airborne Division, nicknamed the "Screaming Eagles." He carried out 26 jumps.

In 1967, England was wearing a red tunic and dancing to the sounds of Sgt. Pepper's Lonely Hearts Club Band

Influenced by San Francisco, in 1967 we had our Summer of Love too.

Protesters and flower children challenged the establishment and rejected the boring, passive lives of their parents. They were also horrified by the monster called the Vietnam War.

Subjected to American bombing, the totalitarian regime of North Vietnam seemed like a brave force of resistance – that image was carefully crafted – while in the South, US-led conventional troops wreaked destruction without ever stopping Viêt-Cong subversion.

The clash of weapons and the voice of protesters were deafening,
drowning out those Vietnamese who dreamed of a pluralistic democracy.

America often wielded a heavy hand in Vietnam, and that triggered a barrage of opposition. We came in for our share of blame too, but as Vietnamese, we suspected our Viêt-Cong adversary was a wolf in sheep's clothing.

ACTION MAN! ACTION SOLDIER! The figure with the moveable limbs was my favorite toy of the times. Domi and I often went to Wimbledon Common in search of real settings for our photos.

Come on, hurry up! The light is perfect!

Yeah, yeah. I just want to fit him with an M16.

One day, we came across a demonstration protesting the war in Vietnam. People had gathered in front of the Vietnamese ambassador's residence – Clockhouse Mansion – located at one end of the Common.

STOP THE BOMBING

STOP THE WAR!

Children are not born to BURN!

HEY! What about VC terrorism?!

DROP ACID NOT BOMBS

MAKE LOVE NOT WAR

Our Action Men inside

Here are two photos that survived from Wimbledon 1967 or 1969. I changed my GIs' uniforms to make them look like Vietnam grunts.

Our Brownie STARFLASH by KODAK (1959).

The Viêt-Cong are FREEDOM FIGHTERS!

What about North-Vietnamese infiltrations along the Ho Chi Minh Trail?!

Later...

Make love, not war!? Just say the word. Ha ha!

Hey, who are these little reactionary fascists?!

Make love not war!

It's no fair, they think the Communists are so pure!

We more or less repeated what our father said.

"The American bombing is a response to Viêt-Cong terrorist activities..."

Bombs away!

VRRRRRRRRRRR

US AIR FORCE

BOM BOM BOM BOM BOM

"When North Vietnam stops its infiltration of men and weapons along the Hô Chi Minh Trail, the Americans will stop their bombing."

But the bombs kill all kinds of innocent civilians. Is that better than what the terrorists do, Papa?

...

It's terrible... but such is war...

I remember a reception at the embassy at Clockhouse Mansion.

Xin mời vào! *

Mmm! We haven't eaten chả giò* in way too long!

Oh, yes! I miss them.

Uh-hem!

Look DISCREETLY at those three children over there.

!!

* Please, come in!
* Often called "nems" – easier to pronounce!

Three Vietnamese children, horribly burned by napalm, were in the care of a couple of British doctors who had worked in Vietnam. What further devastation did their clothes conceal? They were undergoing plastic surgery to repair the damage.

Oh, Jesus!

Holy shit! ---

How horrible!

I hope Mama doesn't see that! She'll have another fit!!

Poor kids!

!

My God!

Mama *did* see the three kids. She was certainly very shocked, but she talked about it soberly in a letter to her parents that *described* the reception.

Among all the beautiful children, most mixed with British mothers, were three kids who were terribly burned by napalm. American warfare at its best. Imagine children without noses or ears, with eyes that scarcely see. Horrible details best not to linger over.

123

NAPALM! That viscous product invented by a Harvard genius was used to great effect in August 1944 on the fortifications of Cézembre, off the coast of Saint-Malo in France.

The German outpost on Cézembre resisted despite twenty-four days of incessant bombing once the city itself was liberated.

Grandma from St-Malo
(Denise)

Mama blamed the Americans for the horrible suffering of the three children. But that was a little too easy. The US was our ally.

Though he'd left the diplomatic service, to make ends meet, Papa still edited the bulletin issued by the Vietnamese embassy in London. The publication told of South Vietnam's accomplishments.

* Republic of Vietnam (the South).

I was all excited by the Colonel's arrival. I'd be able to talk to him about things that my erudite father wasn't interested in.

You're a paratrooper?!! I heard the training was really hard!

It's tough, but if you've got the will ---

Oh, boy! I wonder if they'd accept me---

Well, why not? It's really all in your head, you know.

My cat Felix

Wow! I'd love that!

Later ---

In our newsletter about the South Vietnamese armed forces, let's start by refuting the erroneous and too common idea that the Americans are the ones doing all the fighting.

SCRITCH SCRITCH

I agree!

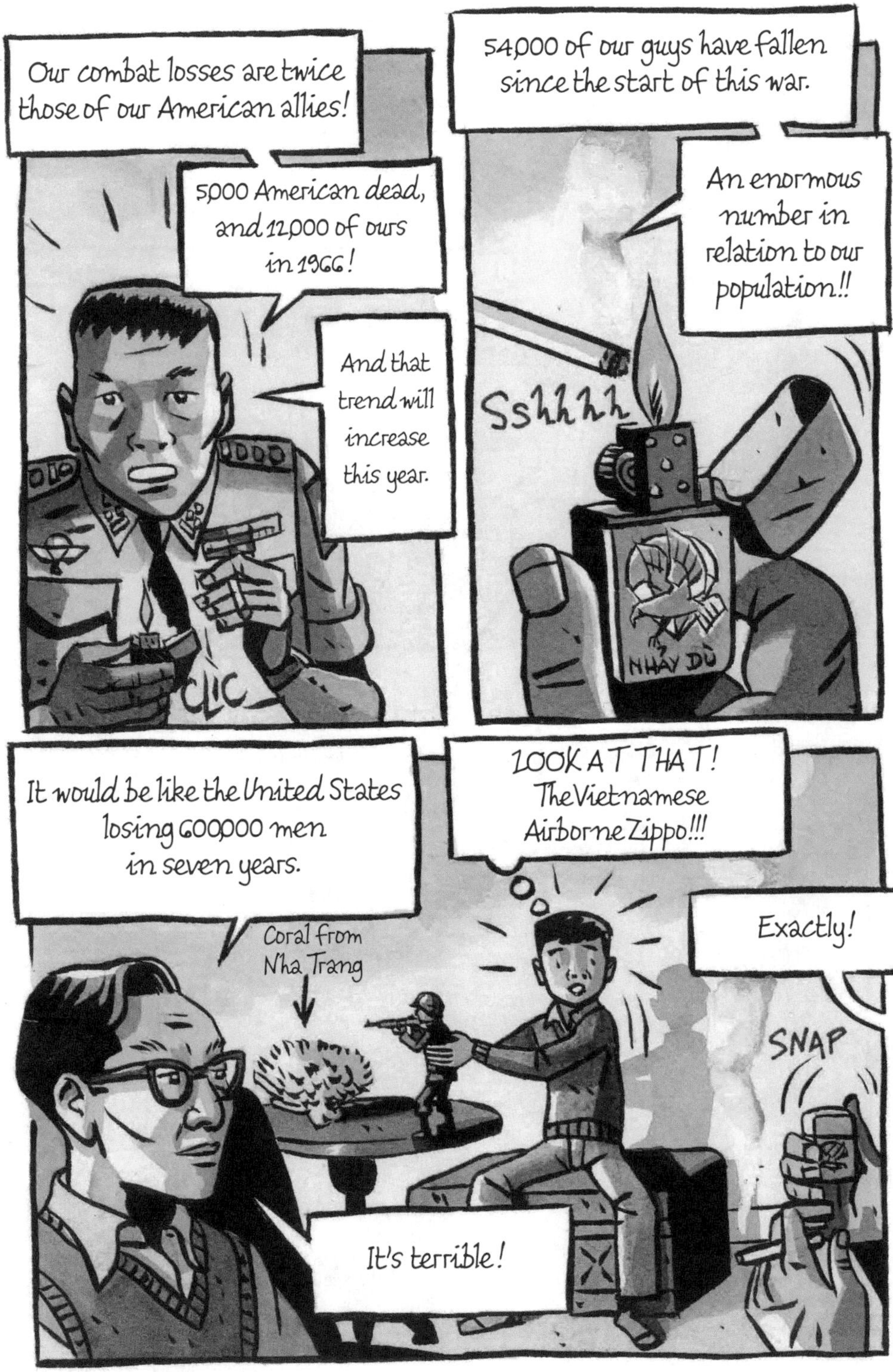
Our combat losses are twice those of our American allies!
5000 American dead, and 12000 of ours in 1966!
And that trend will increase this year.
CLIC
54000 of our guys have fallen since the start of this war.
An enormous number in relation to our population!!
Sshhhh
NHAY DU
It would be like the United States losing 600000 men in seven years.
Coral from Nha Trang
LOOK AT THAT! The Vietnamese Airborne Zippo!!!
Exactly!
SNAP
It's terrible!

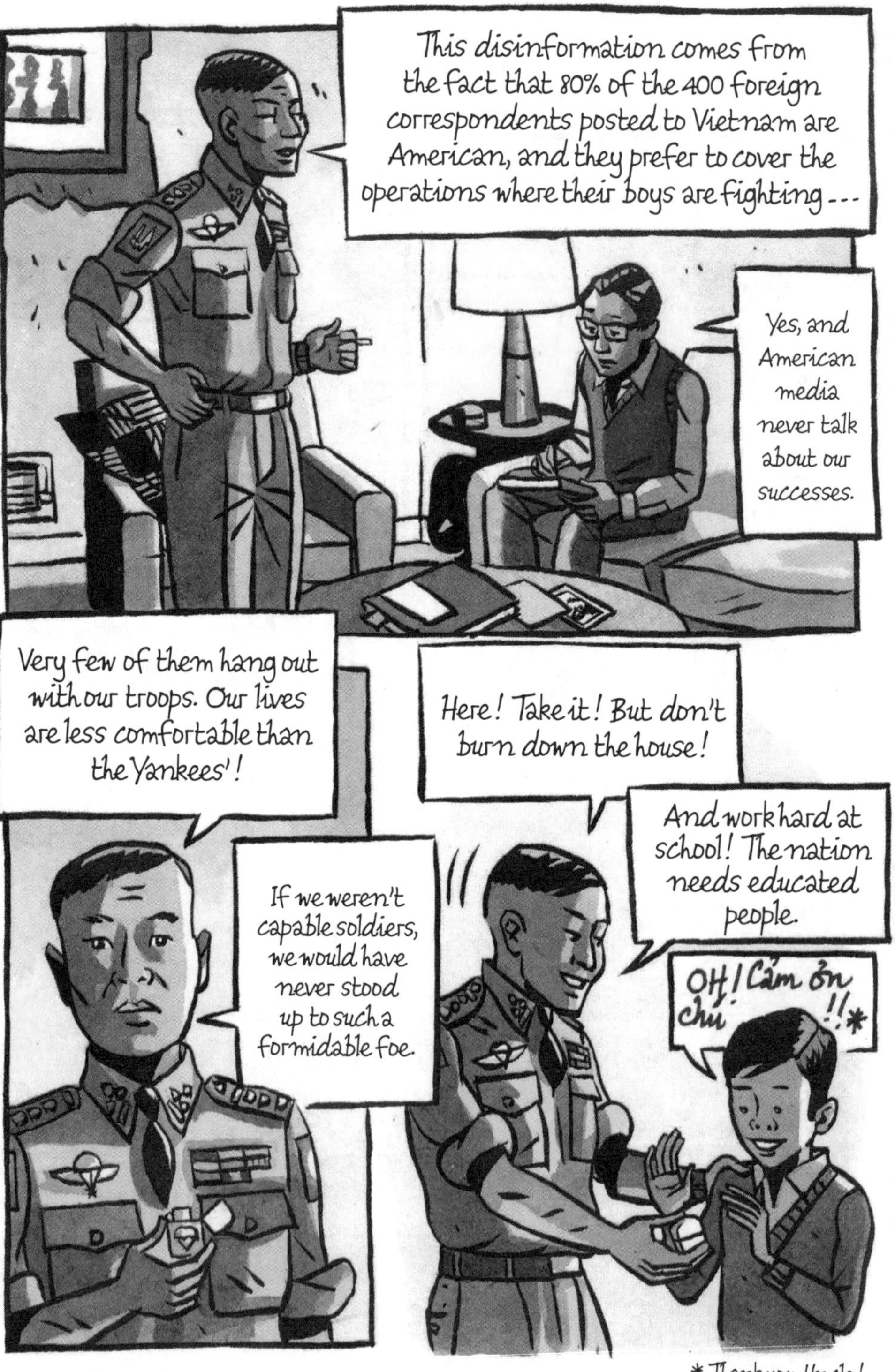
This disinformation comes from the fact that 80% of the 400 foreign correspondents posted to Vietnam are American, and they prefer to cover the operations where their boys are fighting ...
Yes, and American media never talk about our successes.
Very few of them hang out with our troops. Our lives are less comfortable than the Yankees'!
If we weren't capable soldiers, we would have never stood up to such a formidable foe.
Here! Take it! But don't burn down the house!
And work hard at school! The nation needs educated people.
OH! Cảm ơn chú!!*

* Thank you, Uncle!

THE YEAR OF THE MONKEY: 1968

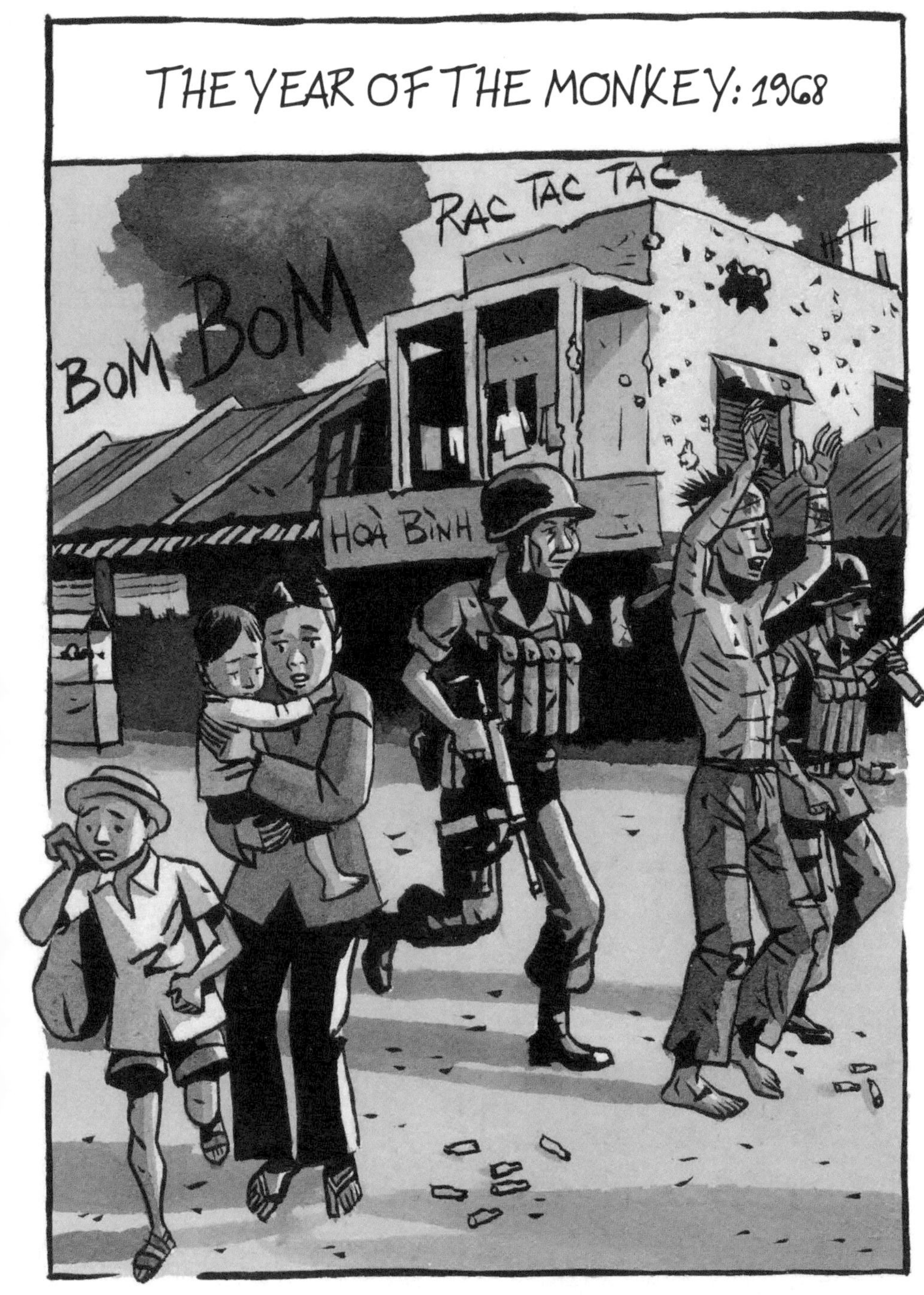
RAC TAC TAC
BOM BOM
HOÀ BÌNH

At the beginning of 1968, our hopes began to rise.

Hai mười năm nhục nhằn đã qua
Hôm nay thấy mặt trời rực sáng— *

What are you singing, Papa?!

It's Trinh Cong Son's new song! A song of peace!

It's fantastic! Vietnamese from the North and the South are going to meet in Paris to discuss making PEACE, sweetheart!

Do you think the war will stop, Papa?

That would be wonderful!!

Sadly, Papa's optimism would soon be betrayed ---

* "Dong Dao Hoà Bình" is a peace song from 1968: "Twenty years of humiliation, shame, and hard labor have passed. Today we see the sun at long last, shining with all its hope ---"

* Têt: the Sino-Vietnamese lunar new year.

131

During the night of January 30, 1968, violating the Tết truce, 85,000 NLF commandos struck at the heart of some one hundred cities in the South.

Over there — at 121 — that's where the puppet lives!

Some VC groups aimed their weapons at strategic points in the cities. Other teams had blacklists with the names of "enemies of the People."

Cruel tyrants and traitors must answer for their crimes against the Revolution!

It was the kick-off for a general offensive orchestrated by Hanoi, and designed to set off an uprising in the South.

Light RPD machine gun

Chinese SKS rifle

* Be careful, that building's full of civilians!

During that same night, January 30, 1968, 6000 North Vietnamese regulars flying the NLF flag* took over the city of Huê, in central Vietnam. The former imperial capital carried a substantial symbolic weight.

* The National Liberation Front, created in the South in 1960, claimed to be independent from Hanoi.
* War cry: Surrender or die!

In Huê as elsewhere, the VC had drawn up lists of "cruel and reactionary tyrants" to be eliminated. There is disagreement over the numbers of executions, but in the month following the battle, some 2,500 bodies were exhumed from mass graves around Huê.

The current authorities, as well as certain historians and journalists, deny these massacres took place, claiming that the dead – some with their hands tied – were from the 1968 Têt offensive. Whatever the reality, many South Vietnamese believed it was true, and began fearing a blood bath if the Communists were victorious.

The fighting to take back Huê lasted 28 days and the city was devastated. Out of an initial population of 140,000, 5,800 were killed and 116,000 found themselves homeless.

In the midst of the clatter of weapons, one shot was heard around the world: the report of a .38 Special.

BANG

General Loan

CLIC CLAC

Nguyễn Văn Lém

Eddie Adams

Eddie Adams, an AP photographer,* captured the decisive moment when General Loan, the chief of the National Police of South Vietnam, executed a VC prisoner in the middle of a Saigon street. The killing provoked indignation and shock.

This won't help South Vietnam's cause at all!

*Associated Press.

Pacifists and leftists pounced on Eddie Adams' photo and made it an icon of Vietnam's "dirty war."

The execution of the VC prisoner was certainly a war crime, but the NLF cadre Nguyen Van Lem had just been caught red-handed at the house of a police colonel, and friend of General Loan's.

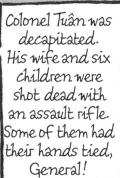

Colonel Tuân was decapitated. His wife and six children were shot dead with an assault rifle. Some of them had their hands tied, General!

Badly wounded during the Tết fighting, Loan had his leg amputated. After 1975, he tried to rebuild his life in the US, but considered a murderer, he was chased out of every city that he tried to settle in. He died of cancer in Virginia in 1998.

During the 1968 Têt offensive that dragged on for nearly five months, city-dwellers were subjected to terrifying rocket fire from Katyusha, 107, 122, and 140 mm shells. These rockets were fired from

That'll teach the civilians to leave the areas liberated by the NLF!

makeshift installations – two hefty sticks in cross formation were enough – from the outskirts of the cities. To avoid being spotted, the VC shot only one or two from any given site. Their trajectory was a matter of chance.

Precision was not an objective. The Viêt-Cong wanted to punish civilians who had taken refuge in areas controlled by the "puppet" administration, and impose a reign of terror. People said that the mere sound of a rocket explosion tore through the heart and twisted the belly.

BLAM

Troi oi !*

Aaaaah !!

In a 2015 report, Amnesty International condemned the use of rockets – indiscriminant munitions – against military targets near civilian areas. (Ref. 21/1178/2015)

* In God's name!

The Tết Offensive decimated the NLF battle force. Of the 85,000 combatants involved, more than 70,000 perished, sent to their deaths by their commanders. After 1968, Hanoi would fill out the ranks of the missing NLF soldiers with North Vietnamese regulars, taking control of the revolutionary southern organization in the process.

Though a military fiasco, the offensive of the Year of the Monkey* was the great turning point in the Vietnam War. It chipped away at the morale of the American people and ended up as a psychological victory.

* Tết Mậu Thân 1968: Tết of the Year of the Monkey.

London, May 1968

The high losses during the Têt offensive are making the war very unpopular in the United States ...

The peace talks open tomorrow in Paris ...

I just hope the Americans won't drop us!

Distraught, LBJ* has announced he would not be running for president in the upcoming elections in the fall

THE NEW YORK TIMES
VIETNAM IN TURMOIL

Papa, I got a cone with a "flake"!*

Good thinking, sweetheart!

* President Lyndon Baines Johnson.
* A chocolate wafer.

140

Were they hoping to inspire the general uprising that was taking its time? Or mark points at the opening of the peace talks, or give Uncle Hô the gift of victory for his 78th birthday on May 19? Whatever the reason, the VC launched major new attacks on May 5 and May 25, 1968.

These "mini-Têt" offensives were even deadlier than the first one in February. The final battles took place among the pagodas in the poor quarters of Saigon, where the VC claimed they were like "a fish in water." The water was blood-red.

From faraway England, we followed the Tết fighting, worried about our family in Vietnam. But for us, life went on normally. On Sunday, we often attended Mass at Notre Dame de France in the heart of Soho, a freewheeling district in the West End.

In the church there was a fresco of the Crucifixion from 1960, signed by the French artist Jean Cocteau.

Wonder if Chu Ba* is still alive.

Hee hee!

Cocteau's Roman soldier is so "in" he's wearing a mini-skirt!

(Sigh)

Papa must have been devastated by the black sun blazing over Vietnam.

My heart is filled with hatred!

Forgive us our tres-passes ---

As we forgive them that trespass against us ---

* Chu Ba was our driver in Saigon from 1961 to 1963. We liked him very much. (See Such a Lovely Little War, 2016.)

143

Much later, in 1991, I learned that four of our cousins in Vietnam had fought for the NLF. The three eldest were foot-soldiers, killed in action in February and March 1968. They were 26, 24, and 20 years old.

The youngest was an artilleryman who was sent back to his parents, badly wounded. The three brothers are resting together in the Martyrs of the Homeland Cemetery in Long Binh, near Saigon, where the soldiers' graves are set in a circle as if around a campfire, symbolized by a shrub.

THEY KNOW NOT WHAT THEY DO

At the end of 1969, our Vietnamese grandparents came and spent a month with us in London, their first and last visit.

Damn, Bà Nôi* only speaks Vietnamese and I've forgotten everything.

Don't worry, Mireille, Ông Nôi speaks French.

With us, Bà Nôi's first language was cooking.

Oh, this good smell reminds me of Saigon, it really brings me back!

It's chicken with ginger sauce. I should learn that recipe!

Far out!

Mmm! Smells good!

flower shirt

* Ông and Bà Nôi: paternal grandfather and grandmother.

Here comes a plane from the Saigon puppet regime!

Without using a pattern, Bà Nội could sew a Vietnamese tunic.

Bà phải may tay áo ngắn lên cho con! *

Đẹp quá! *

*I'll have to shorten the sleeve.
* It's really pretty!

147

Richmond Park, London

Hỏi Tết Mậu-Thân chắc là kinh hoàng lắm, phải không, cha? *

Yes, Khánh, we were sweating! The worst was when the VC shot rockets.

I need a smoke!

Drea on!

The NLF attacks the cities to keep peasants from fleeing the countryside that's under their control – cynical!

Ha! You think that's any better than the Americans and their "free fire zones"?

They fire on anything that moves in NLF-dominated areas. You realize that?!

* The Tết Mậu Thân must have been terrifying, Papa.

148

Be careful with your arrows, Marco!

Yeah, yeah, Mama, don't worry!

rubber glove for dishes

garden stakes

Yes, it's awful!

The excesses and blunders of the American war machine cause general indignation. Our cause has been completely discredited.

Hmm --- Sooner or later, America will give up and pull out of the fight --- We'll be up against our Communist enemies on our own, and they know how to hide their intentions. We saw that during the French Indochina war. They're very clever!

LOOK! A DEER!!

Our Saigon Grandpa had been a schoolteacher, and this was our Vietnamese grandparents' first trip to the West.

WRIGLEY'S
WRIGREY'S →
CHEWING GUM
CHEWING GUM
Scotch Ales YOUN

TOM JONES
AT THE HAYMARKET

Were you and Bà Nội in your house in Gia Dinh during the Tết Offensive in '68?

Yes, Marco. The one all of you lived in when you came to Saigon in 1961.

Did you see any Viêt-Cong guerrillas?

I'm afraid so! One night a group of VC came into our yard.

Ha ha! Did the VC use the WC?

Christmas Greetings Carnaby Street

It was during the second wave of attacks: the "mini-Têt." Bullets were flying everywhere!

Was that in May '68?

Yes!

Right on! The streets belong to the people!

OJD 903E

Lord Jo

PoP

maxi coat (long)

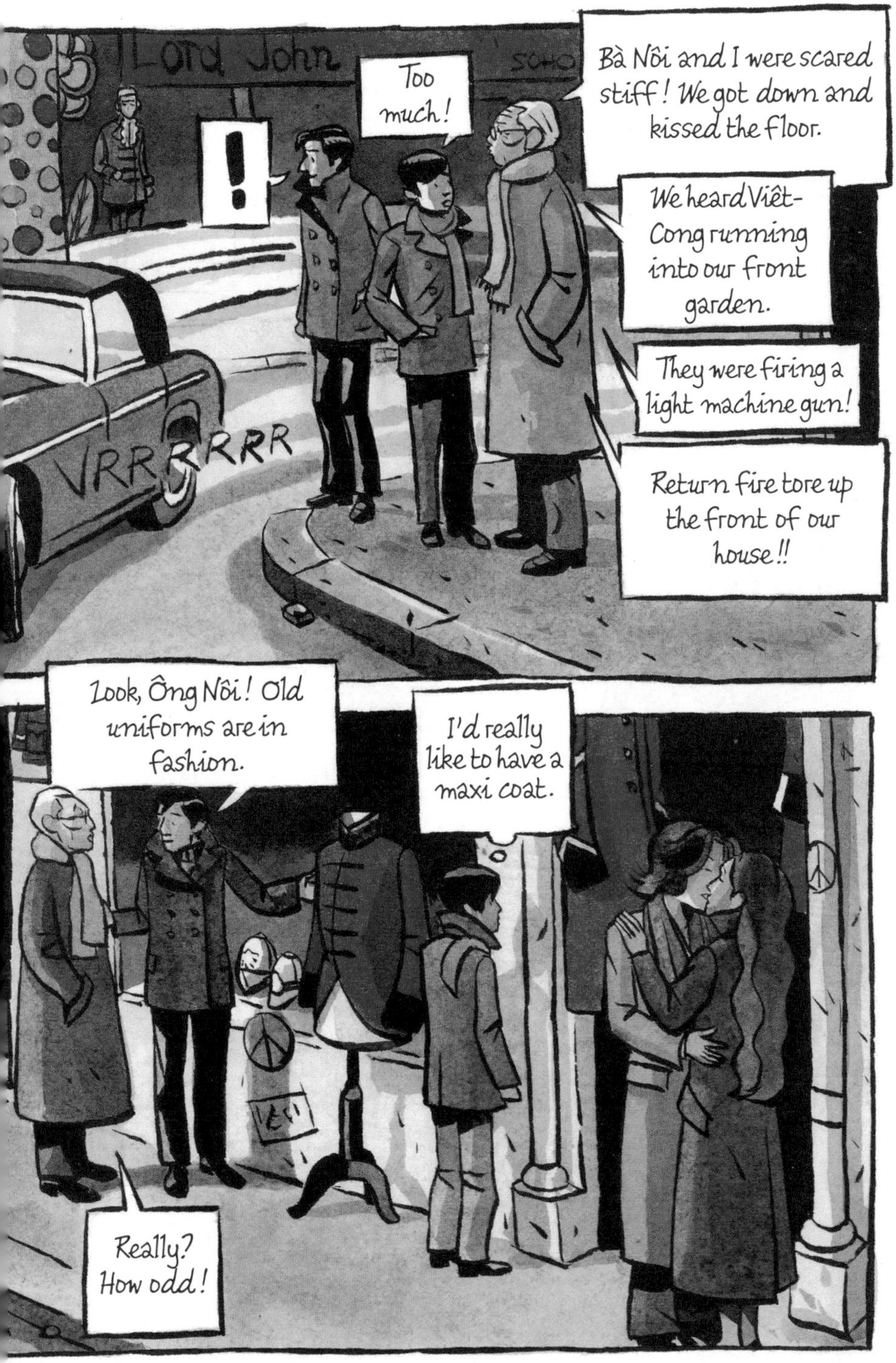

Lord John
SOHO
Bà Nôi and I were scared stiff! We got down and kissed the floor.
Too much!
!
We heard Việt-Cong running into our front garden.
They were firing a light machine gun!
Return fire tore up the front of our house!!
VRRRRRRR
Look, Ông Nôi! Old uniforms are in fashion.
I'd really like to have a maxi coat.
Really? How odd!

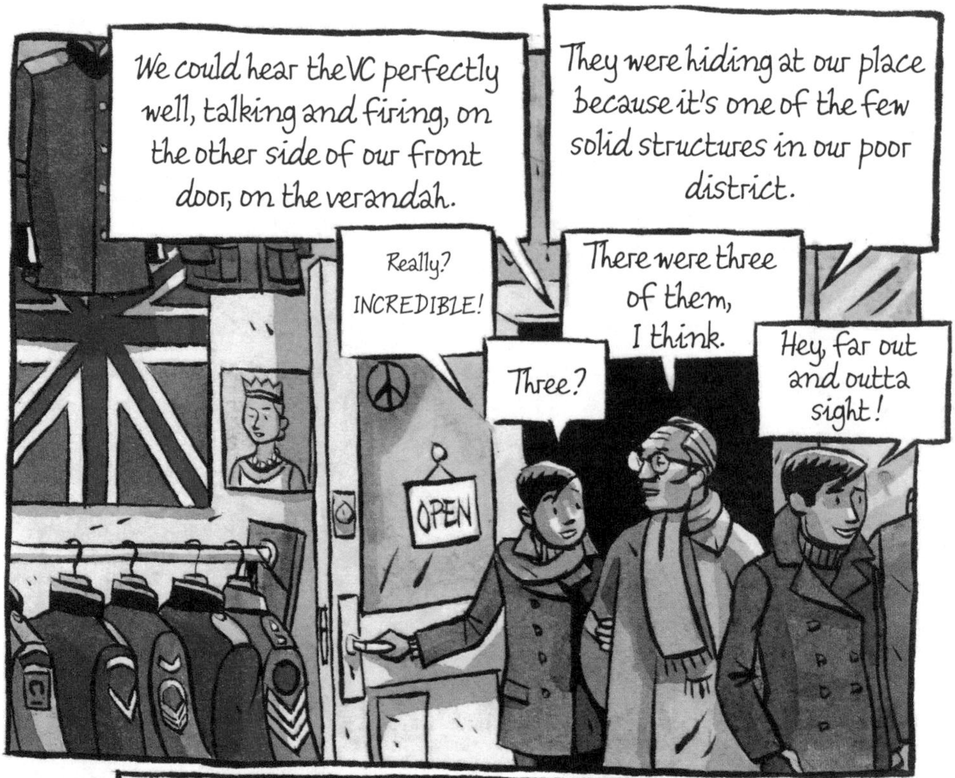
We could hear the VC perfectly well, talking and firing, on the other side of our front door, on the verandah.
They were hiding at our place because it's one of the few solid structures in our poor district.
Really? INCREDIBLE!
There were three of them, I think.
Three?
Hey, far out and outta sight!
OPEN

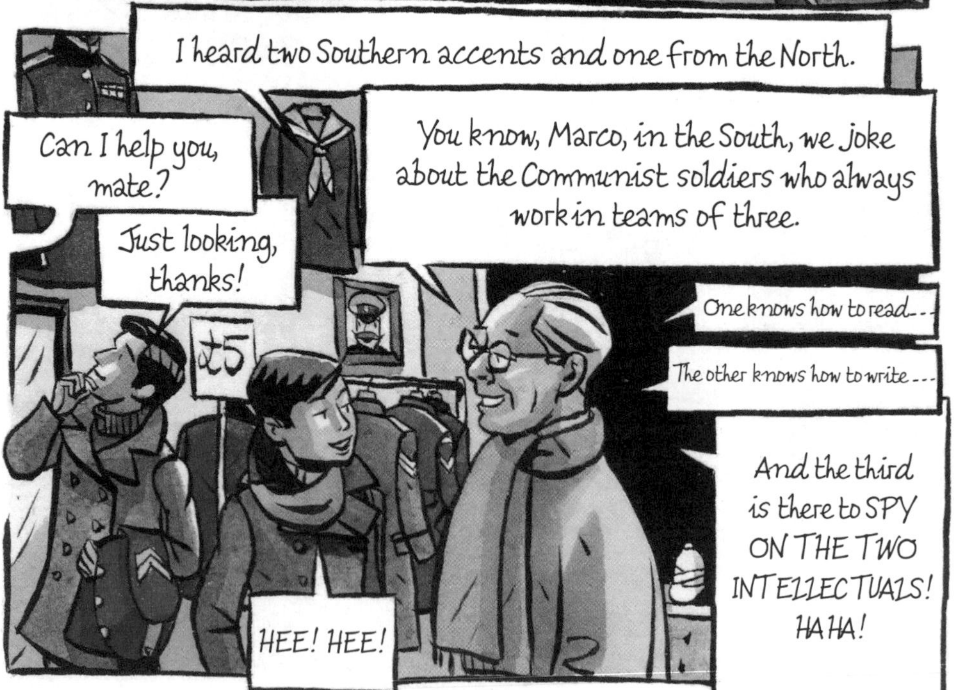
I heard two Southern accents and one from the North.
Can I help you, mate?
You know, Marco, in the South, we joke about the Communist soldiers who always work in teams of three.
Just looking, thanks!
£5
One knows how to read...
The other knows how to write...
And the third is there to SPY ON THE TWO INTELLECTUALS! HA HA!
HEE! HEE!

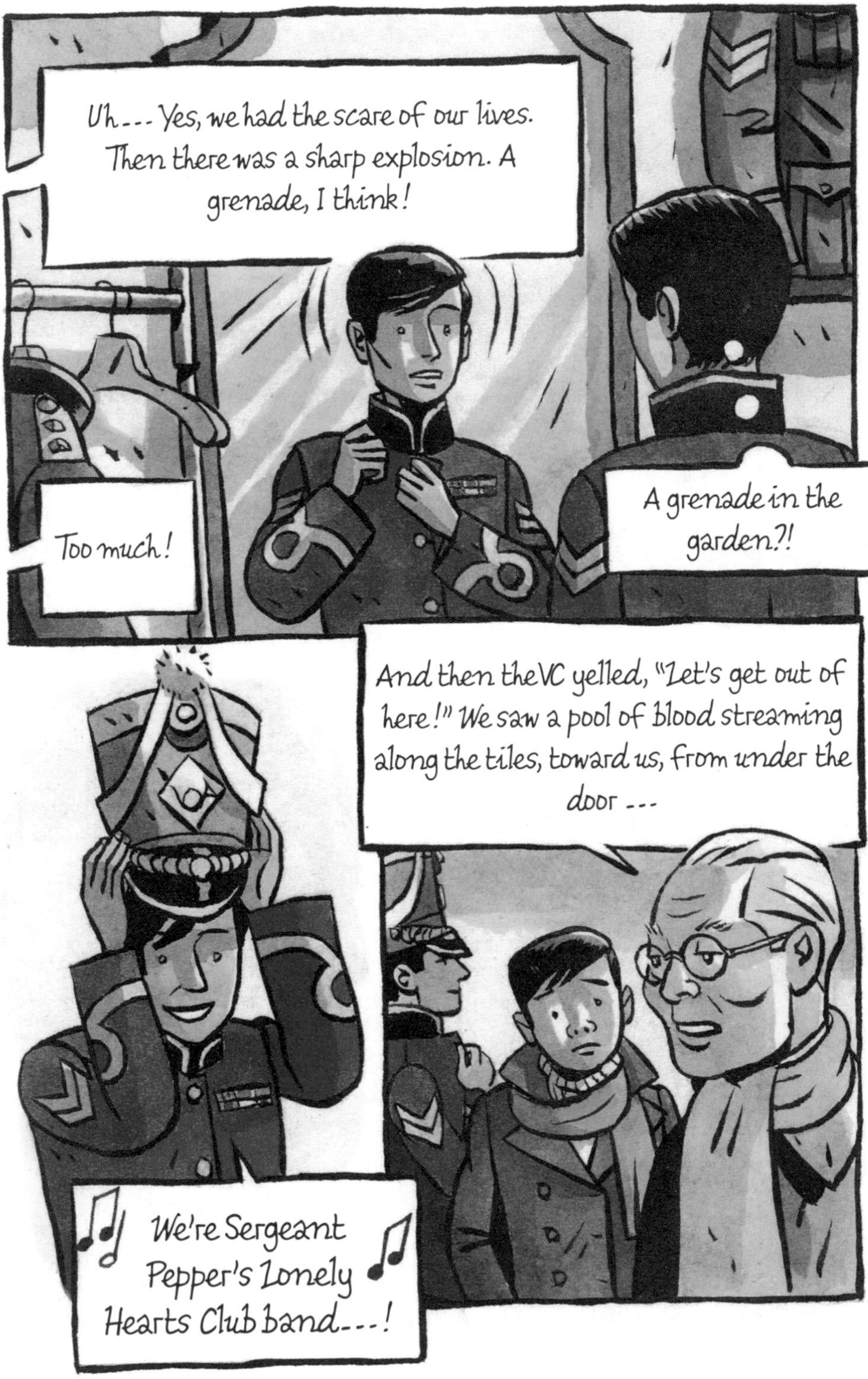
Uh--- Yes, we had the scare of our lives. Then there was a sharp explosion. A grenade, I think!
Too much!
A grenade in the garden?!
And then the VC yelled, "Let's get out of here!" We saw a pool of blood streaming along the tiles, toward us, from under the door ---
We're Sergeant Pepper's Lonely Hearts Club band---!

Little by little, the shooting grew more distant. We smelled smoke. The huts must have been burning ...

DẠ CÓ AI TRONG NAY KHÔNG ?! *

A child's voice was calling: "Is anyone there?" We were shaking, we decided to go out the back. The pool of blood coming from under the front door was spreading.

CÓ AI TRONG NAY KHÔNG?!

?!

* Is anyone in there?

When we went into the little garden that was completely destroyed, we saw the strangest boy--

CLIC
CLAC

Are you hurt, my child?

Ồ, con xin lỗi Ông Bà! Con tưởng nhà hông có ai?!*

Just a scratch! The paratroopers made me a bandage!

* Pardon me, sir, ma'am, I thought the house was empty!

157

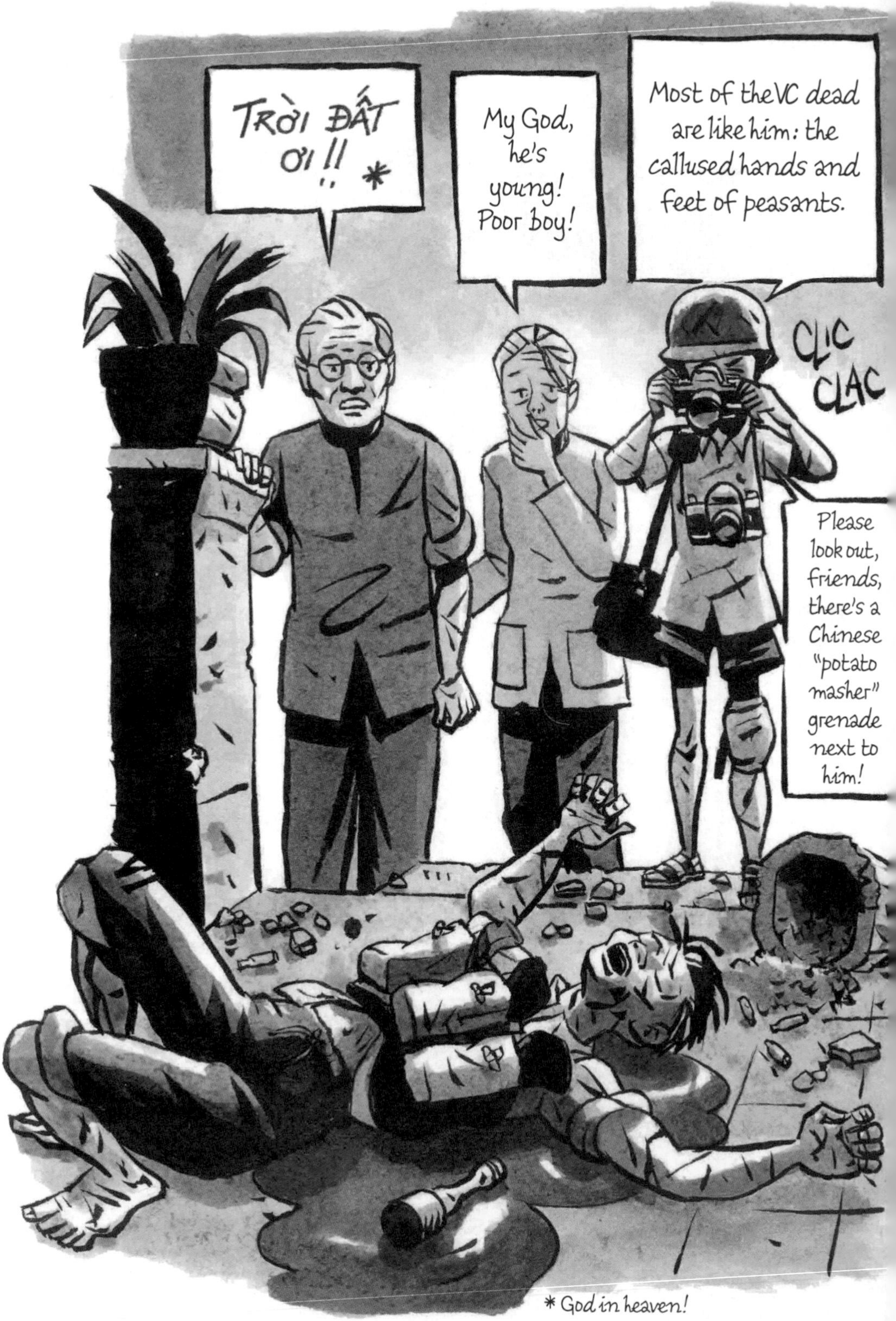
TRỜI ĐẤT ƠI!! *
My God, he's young! Poor boy!
Most of the VC dead are like him: the callused hands and feet of peasants.
CLIC CLAC
Please look out, friends, there's a Chinese "potato masher" grenade next to him!

* God in heaven!

Really, son, aren't you a little young to be doing such a dangerous job?

I've been doing it for two years now!

I also do weddings, parties, sports ---

My father Lô Vinh* is a photo-journalist, but he got wounded, so I'm helping out ---

There's eight of us kids. I'm the oldest — I'm twelve!

Here, son, drink this. It's lemonade.

Oh, thanks Bà!

He's a good boy! His parents can be proud of him.

Ha! We're standing here chatting next to a corpse and the neighborhood is burning!

IT'S MADNESS!

* Lô Vinh was 58 in 1968. Born in the North, he chose to begin life anew in South Vietnam after the 1954 partitioning of the country.

Just then, some young Vietnamese Marines pulling the garbage disposal cart came down our alley. They were picking up the bodies of the VC dead killed in Gia Dinh. They threw ours into their horrible open hearse! He couldn't have been more than 16. What a sad end!

The little reporter went after them like a shot.

I ran behind and called, "WHAT'S YOUR NAME, LITTLE BIG MAN?"

CON TÊN HÙNG!

LỖ MẠNH HÙNG!

* My name's Lỗ Mạnh Hùng!

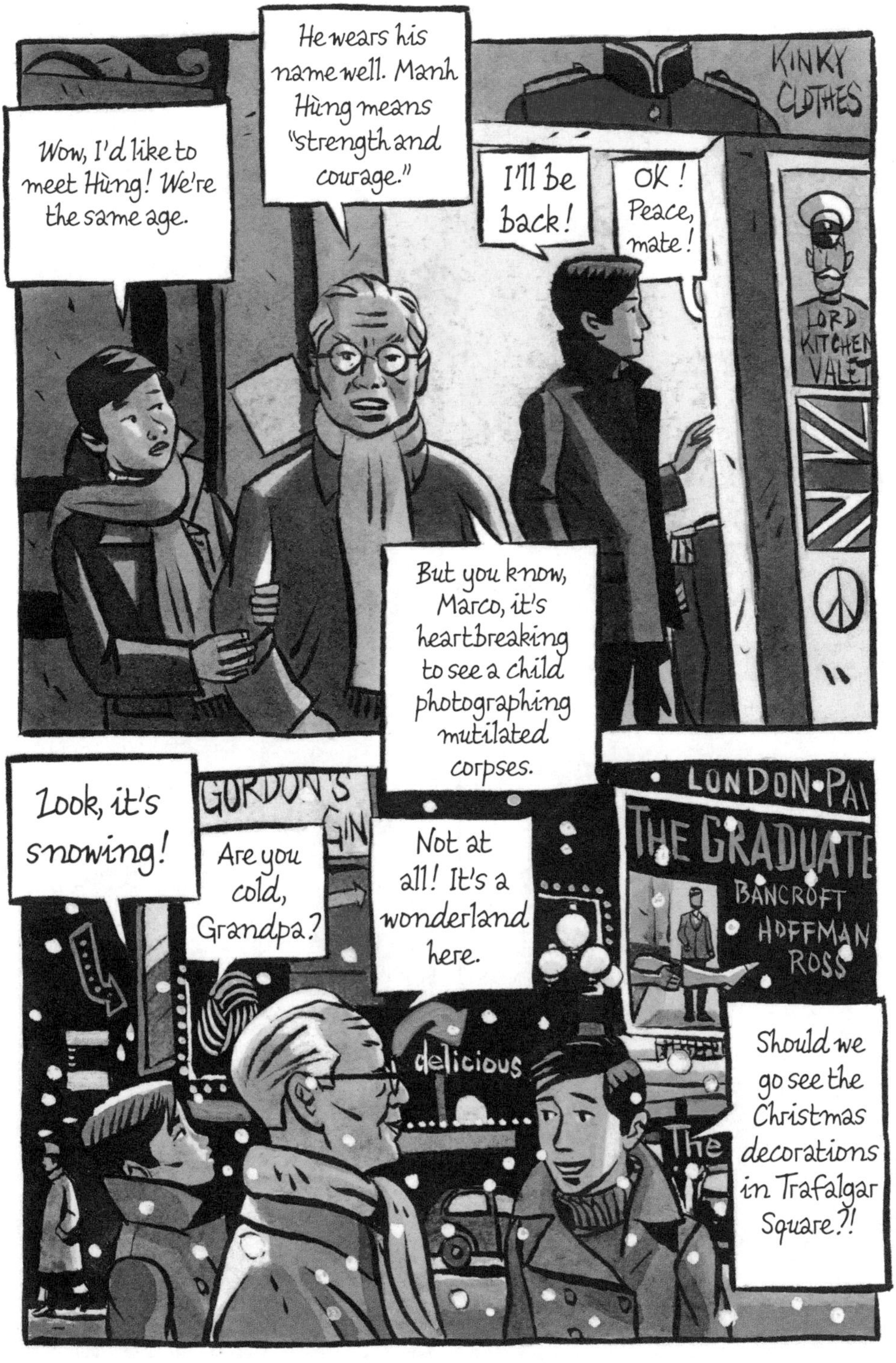
KINKY CLOTHES
Wow, I'd like to meet Hùng! We're the same age.
He wears his name well. Manh Hùng means "strength and courage."
I'll be back!
OK! Peace, mate!
LORD KITCHEN VALET
But you know, Marco, it's heartbreaking to see a child photographing mutilated corpses.
Look, it's snowing!
GORDON'S GIN
Are you cold, Grandpa?
Not at all! It's a wonderland here.
LONDON·PA
THE GRADUATE
BANCROFT
HOFFMAN
ROSS
delicious
Should we go see the Christmas decorations in Trafalgar Square?!

The famous Nelson's Column! Horatio Nelson!

His first name makes me think of "Horace," the Corneille play.

Curiatius, his enemy, says to him ---

"We are but one blood, and one people in two cities ---

Why should we tear ourselves by civil wars?"*

That's what's happening in Vietnam, Ông Nôi!

Why this poster, "VICTORY FOR THE VIÊT-CONG"?!

!

HUM!

Uh--- There are a lot of demonstrations in Trafalgar.

In the West, Grandpa, lots of people support the Viêt-Cong!

They know not what they do ---

*Curiace, HORACE, I, 3. Pierre Corneille, 1640.

162

MAKE LOVE, NOT WAR

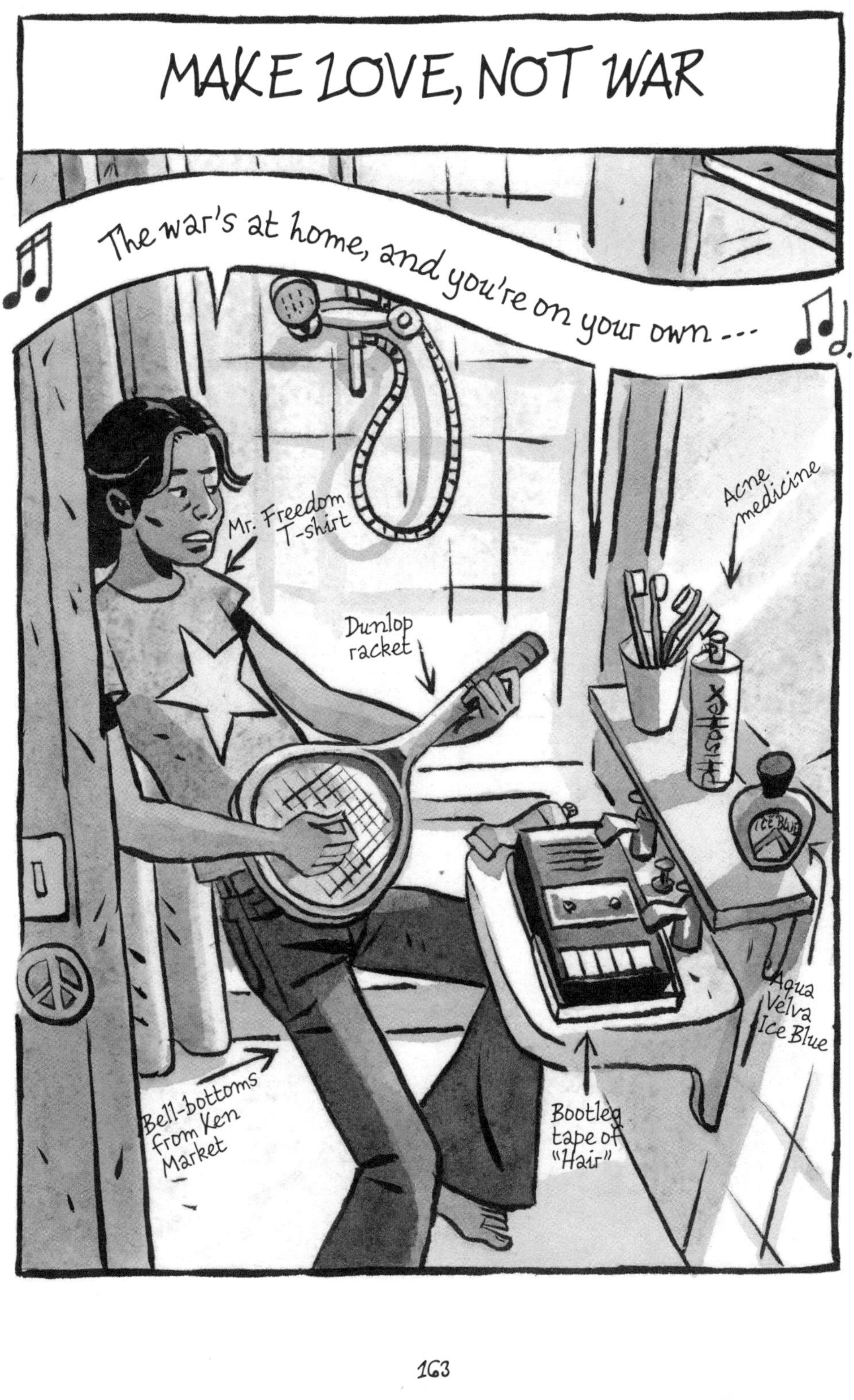

The war's at home, and you're on your own ...
Mr. Freedom T-shirt
Dunlop racket
Acne medicine
Aqua Velva Ice Blue
Bootleg tape of "Hair"
Bell-bottoms from Ken Market

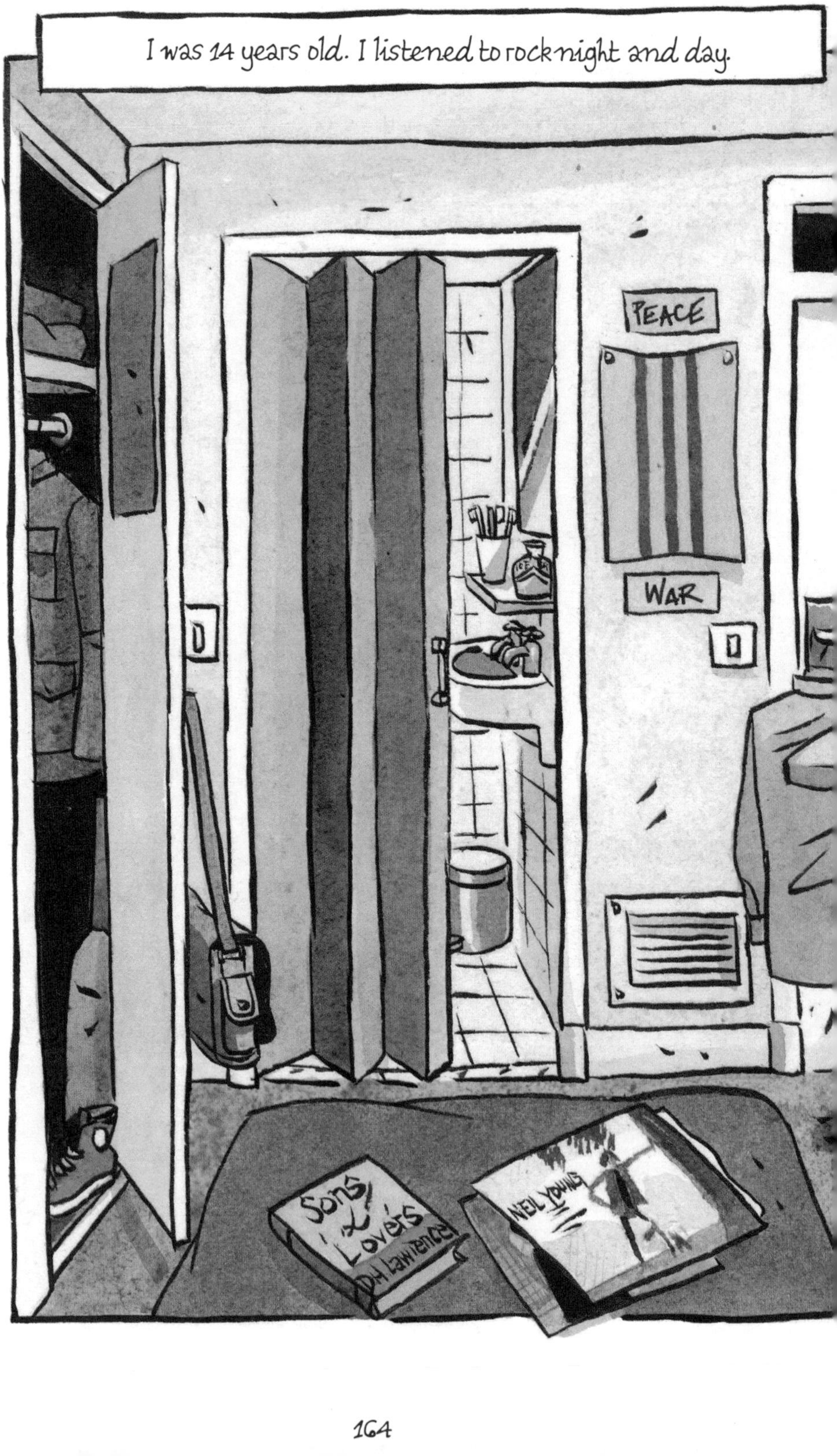
I was 14 years old. I listened to rock night and day.
PEACE
WAR
Sons & Lovers
DH Lawrence
NEIL YOUNG

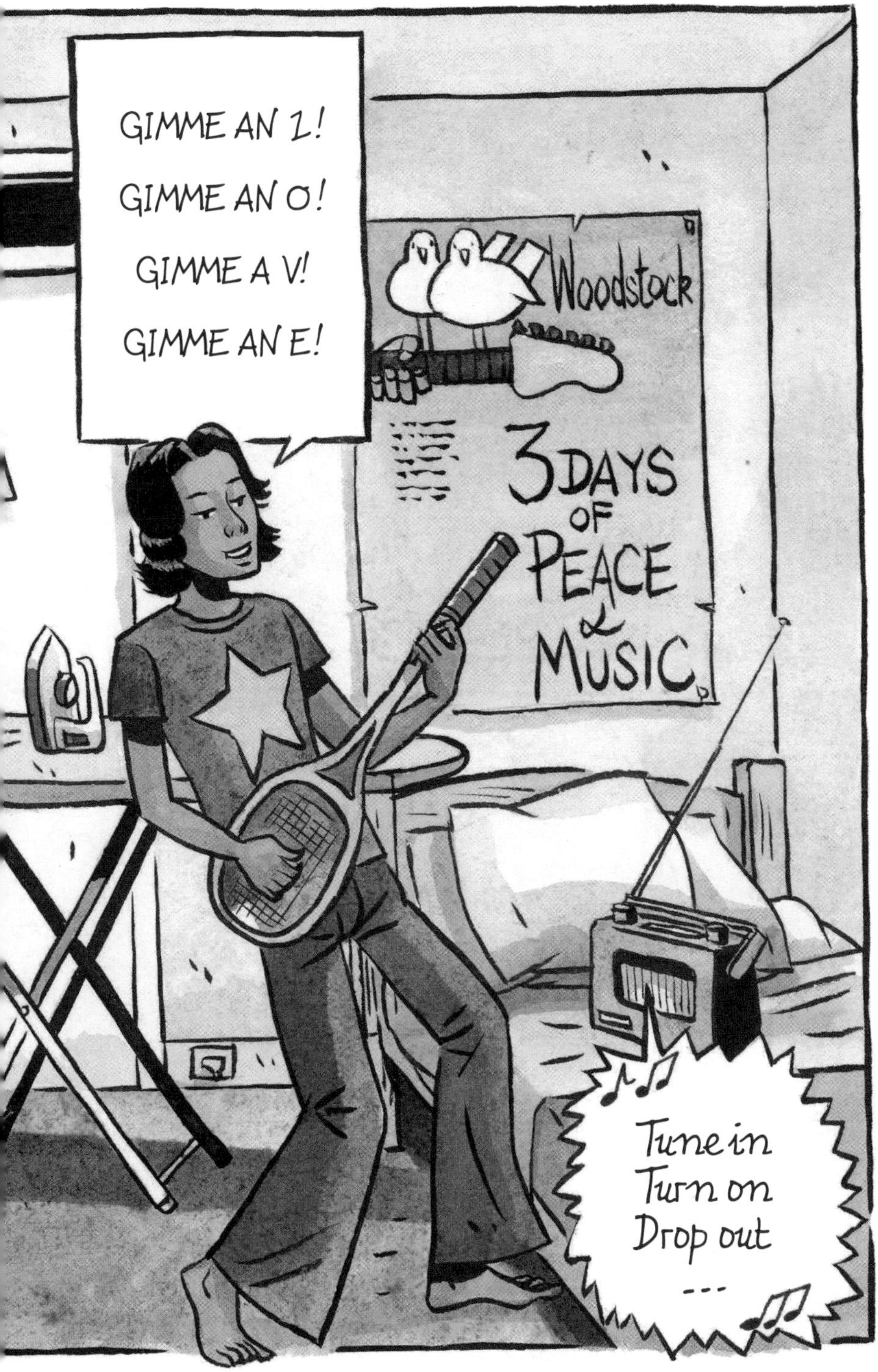
GIMME AN L!
GIMME AN O!
GIMME A V!
GIMME AN E!
Woodstock
3 DAYS OF PEACE & MUSIC
Tune in
Turn on
Drop out
...

I fell in love twice a day ...

Mignonne, allons voir si la rose ... *

It's from the BIBA boutique.

I love their stuff!

I saw the Jeff Beck gig at the LYCEUM last night !*

Lucky bastard !

* See, my lovely, hath not the rose ..." À Cassandre," Pierre de Ronsard, 1524-1585.

I perfected my look at Ken Market, a hip counter-culture bazaar on High Street Kensington ...

Yes, that scarf looks really cool on you, dear!

Indian scarves

... and took my place in the fashion show in the main hall and the corridors at the French Lycée.

Did you watch Monty Python last night, Joanne?

'course! Soooo funny! Hilarious!

WAY IN

Being in London in 1971-72 meant parties in grand Georgian mansions with the beautiful people from the Lycée.

Wow! Very posh!

Happy birthday, Bettina!

Oh, how sweet of you, Marco!

« Mud Slide Slim », James Taylor

Often the game was fixed.

I think Joanne fancies you!*

Oh really ?!

Strong scent of Aqua Velva

DING DONG

Wow, I've got a shot with JOANNE!

Oh Antonia! Amaury!

Indian scarf

No jiving like in France. In London, it was "freak out."

♪ You're blowin' my soul You're messin' ♪ my mind, oh Babe!

Joanne

The slow dances let you check out the truth behind the rumors.

♪ ♪ Ooh, if you love me don't make me wait ♪♪

What do I do now? Kiss her?

Only one problem: I had to be home by midnight. No fair!

Shit! I gotta go!

I had to run to catch the last train ---

The endless landscape of the gray London suburbs ---

SKINS! RULE

RATTLE RATTLE RATTLE RATTLE

I thought of Joanne's lips --- JOANNE ---

"Je fais souvent ce rêve étrange et penetrant ---"*

RATTLE RATTLE

* I often have this strange and penetrating dream---" Paul Verlaine, French poet, 1844-1896, "Mon rêve familier."

The week after the party at Bettina's, Joanne let on that I was a little clingy, maybe more than a little---

Pass, Philip, pass!!

Marco--- (SIGH) Why don't you play football like the other boys?---

Instead of hanging out with the girls all the time?

Uh--- Well, I'm useless at football ...

← Burberry trench coat

Later, I bought a pack of ten Player's No 6 from a vending machine.

Why don't I play football?

Why do I hang out with girls all the time?

Football bores me and I think Joanne's pretty --- But this cigarette tastes like crap ---

I had lots of friends in London: Clive, Bruce, Arnold, Philip, Jean-Jacques, just to name a few. I envied their freedom.

Anyway, it would have been hard to see Joanne outside of school ---

My mother's a drag. She keeps us caged up!

Jack Bruce, the bass player from Cream, is playing in Hyde Park Sunday. You coming?

When their kids become teenagers, it's usually a trial for the parents, but my mother, who couldn't keep up with me, reacted badly.

Mama, on Sunday can I go to a free rock concert in Hyde Park?

WHAT? Another party with girls?

Ha! Nothing but drugged-out hippies at those concerts! You'd be better off at the Common.

NO! Not at all, it's with Clive!

The counter-culture was at its peak at the beginning of the seventies. Sometimes our parents made an effort to keep pace.

In 1970, Papa and Mama saw Dennis Hopper's cult film, "Easy Rider," about drugs, free love, freedom, the open road, and the confrontation with conservative America.

No man, this is grass!

You mean marijuana?

Here's what Mama wrote to her parents in Saint-Malo: "Last night we went to see a hippie film at our local cinema, 'Easy Rider,' which was X-rated, restricted to those 16 and older. The theater was full of black leather jackets – frightful young people – who are usually on the backs of their large motorcycles preaching violence as a way of fighting another type of young people's philosophy, just as revolting with its laziness and drug use: the hippies, whose symbols are flowers and love."

A telling story about my mother and '69, "the year of Eros," according to French singer/songwriter Serge Gainsbourg. One day, when I came back from Lycée, she yelled at me, almost hysterical, for having brought home a 45 rpm record, a scandalous piece of music that she must have spent the afternoon listening to. It was "Je t'aime--- moi non plus," the famous bedroom duet between Gainsbourg and Jane Birkin.

FREAK OUT!

Hari hari! Biphale janama gonainu *

* O Lord Hari! I have spent my life uselessly. "Heart on Fire," traditional Indian song.

The hedonism of the Swinging Sixties didn't make our parents' job any easier. Our education was the result of both of their two cultures, Vietnamese and French.

Jeez, is Papa ever serious! Work and read, that's all he does!

A regular priest!

Yeah, he wants us to be like the VC.

They're noble and virtuous!

VRRRRRRRRRRRR

HEEEEELP!

Mireille was lucky to get out and go to university in Durham.

Yeah!! Papa and especially Mama were super-strict with her!

Carnival music

I remember. I hope Mama will let me go see Mireille with you!

No FLIRTING before marriage, Mad Mom would tell her!

Fitted shirt

The "Helter Skelter" ride at Wimbledon Common

In 1971, for Easter holiday, Dominique and I took the INTERCITY train to Durham, 400 kilometers away in northeast England.

Mireille was two years into studying philosophy and political science at Durham. She had joined the liberation train.

Peace! I'm Chris.

Here come the little brothers!

Laura Ashley dress

How's it going at the house with Mama? Not too tough?

Oh, she's always freaking out!

And Noëlle?! I miss her!

And Papa?

Still as cute and cool as ever!

She turned nine in January.

He flipped out 'cause I'm flunking out of lycée.

Oh, Domi! School's not your thing, I guess.

VRRRRRRRR

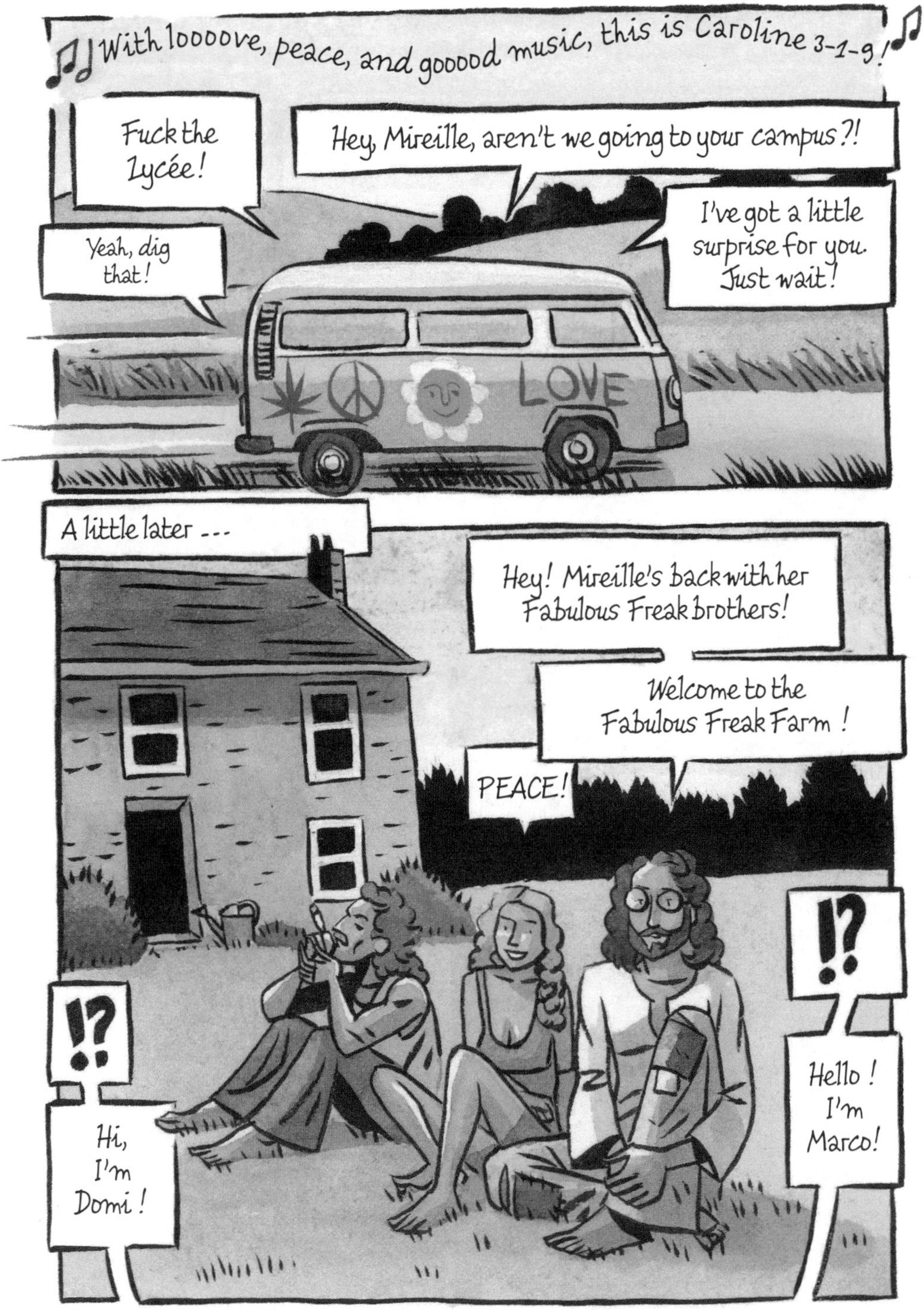
With loooove, peace, and gooood music, this is Caroline 3-1-9!
Fuck the Lycée!
Yeah, dig that!
Hey, Mireille, aren't we going to your campus?!
I've got a little surprise for you. Just wait!
LOVE
A little later ...
Hey! Mireille's back with her Fabulous Freak brothers!
Welcome to the Fabulous Freak Farm!
PEACE!
!?
!?
Hi, I'm Domi!
Hello! I'm Marco!

The Fabulous Furry Freak Brothers were a cast of characters created by the American comic artist Gilbert Shelton. We came across several collections in Mireille's commune.

I'm gonna slip out and play with my friends and fornicate and fight in the yard!

Ha Ha Ha!

Hee hee!

Fat Freddy's Cat is too much!

Like Shelton's freaks, the Durham hippies didn't do much outside of smoking grass and hash and listening to music, and maybe going for a walk in the fields in search of cow pies where hallucinogenic mushrooms grew, not to mention making love and not war in a haze of patchouli.

Hey, you're exaggerating! We make candles and sell them to freaks so we can buy grass!

180

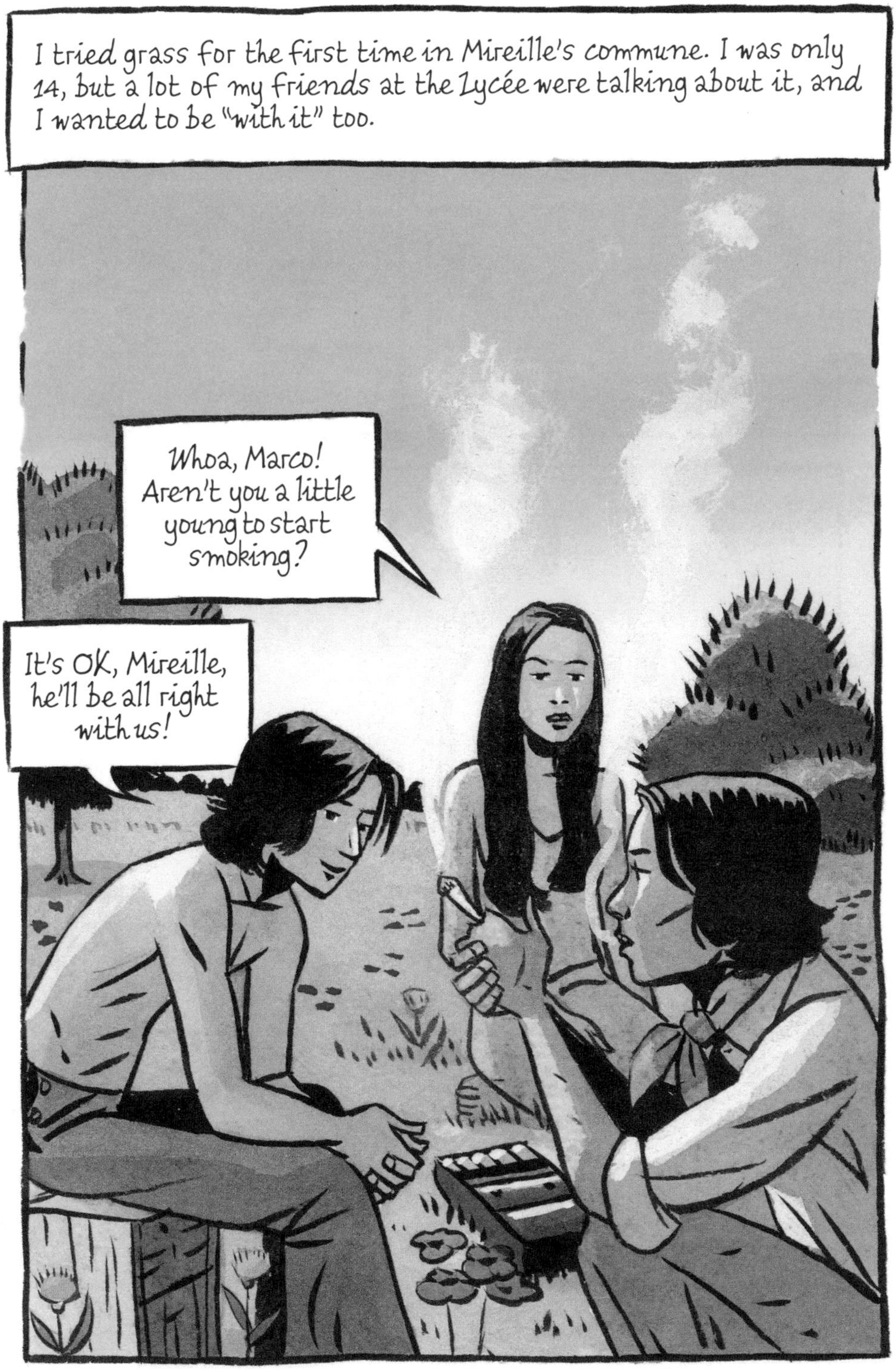
I tried grass for the first time in Mireille's commune. I was only 14, but a lot of my friends at the Lycée were talking about it, and I wanted to be "with it" too.
Whoa, Marco! Aren't you a little young to start smoking?
It's OK, Mireille, he'll be all right with us!

I didn't have to wait long for the grass to kick in.

You okay, Marco?

Yeah, yeah. Cool!

I started noticing things I'd never paid attention to.

Bzzz

Bzzzzzzzz

I remember listening to a cassette of the musical "Hair" that day. The pot made me hear a tune the way I'd never imagined it before.

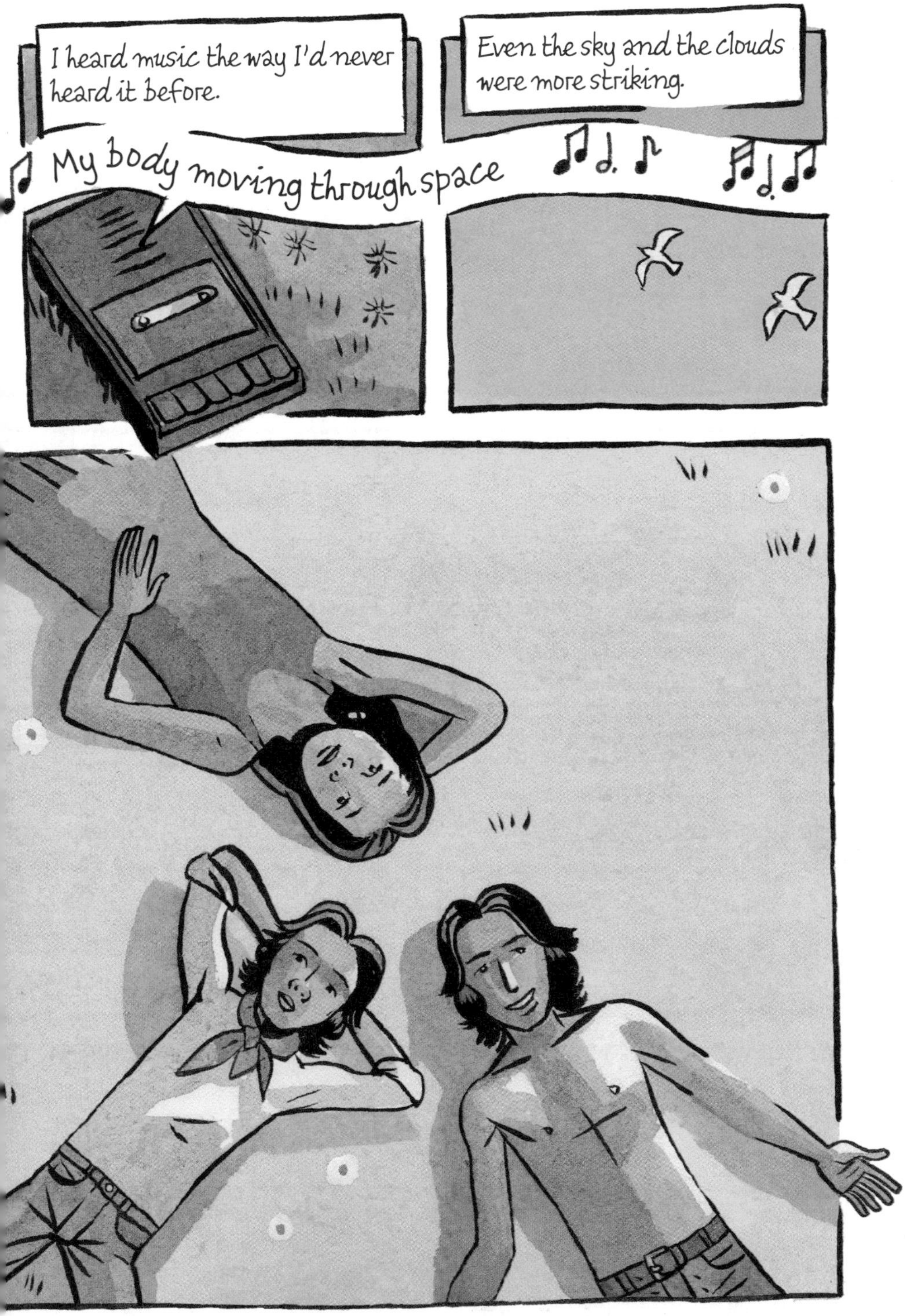
I heard music the way I'd never heard it before.
Even the sky and the clouds were more striking.
My body moving through space

I listened to "3-5-0-0," a song about the Vietnam War and its horrors. The images came to me all too clearly ---

A bird flying overhead turning into a B-52 --

 FLAP FLAP FLAP FLAP

 VRRRRR

Bullets whizzing past WHIIIZZZZ

 ... The glint of bayo

Shrapnel and torn-off limbs ---

 THROB THROB

WHHHIIIRRR

Guns and ammo ---

 COLT .223.

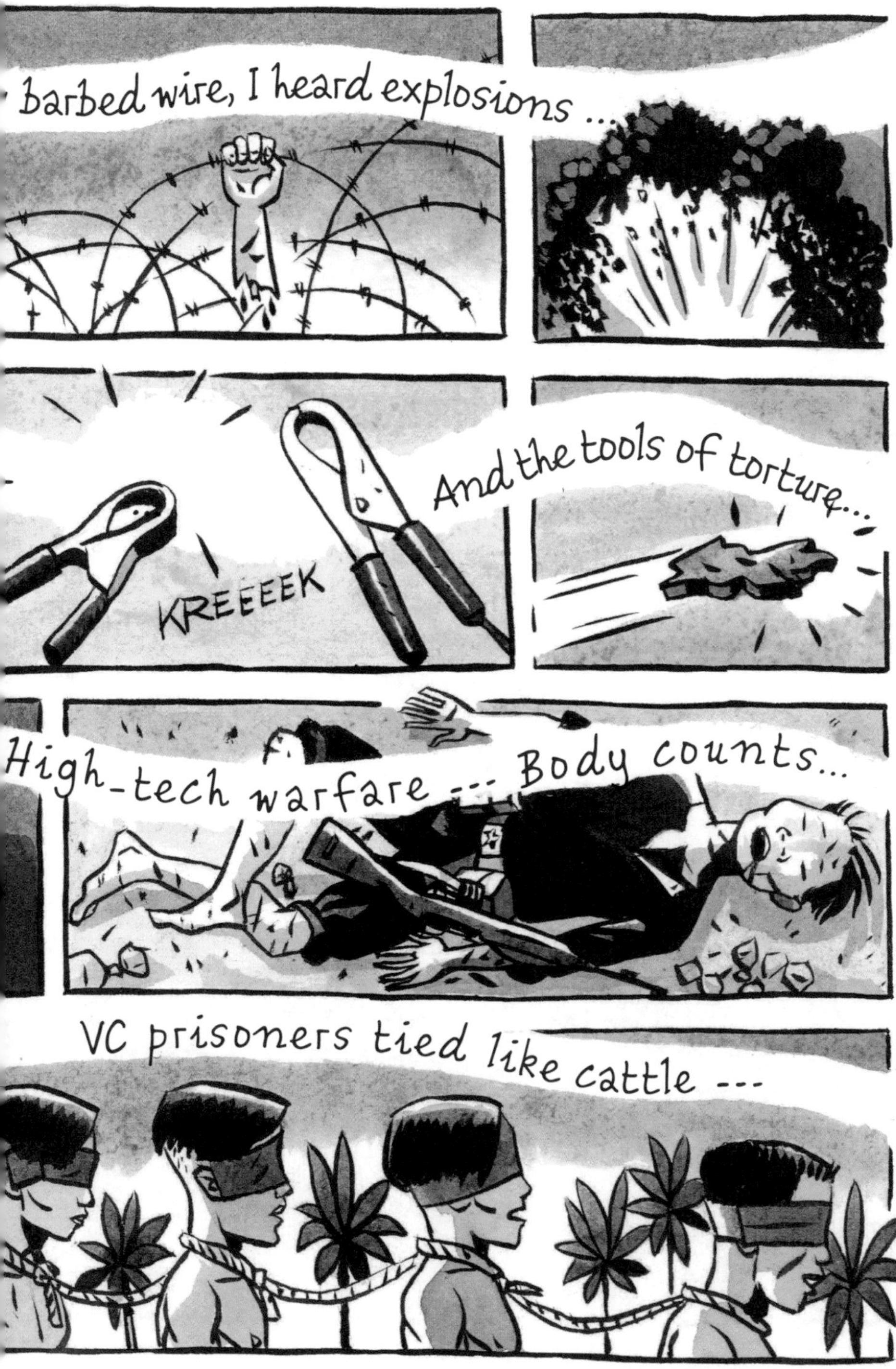
barbed wire, I heard explosions ...
And the tools of torture...
KREEEEK
High-tech warfare --- Body counts...
VC prisoners tied like cattle ---

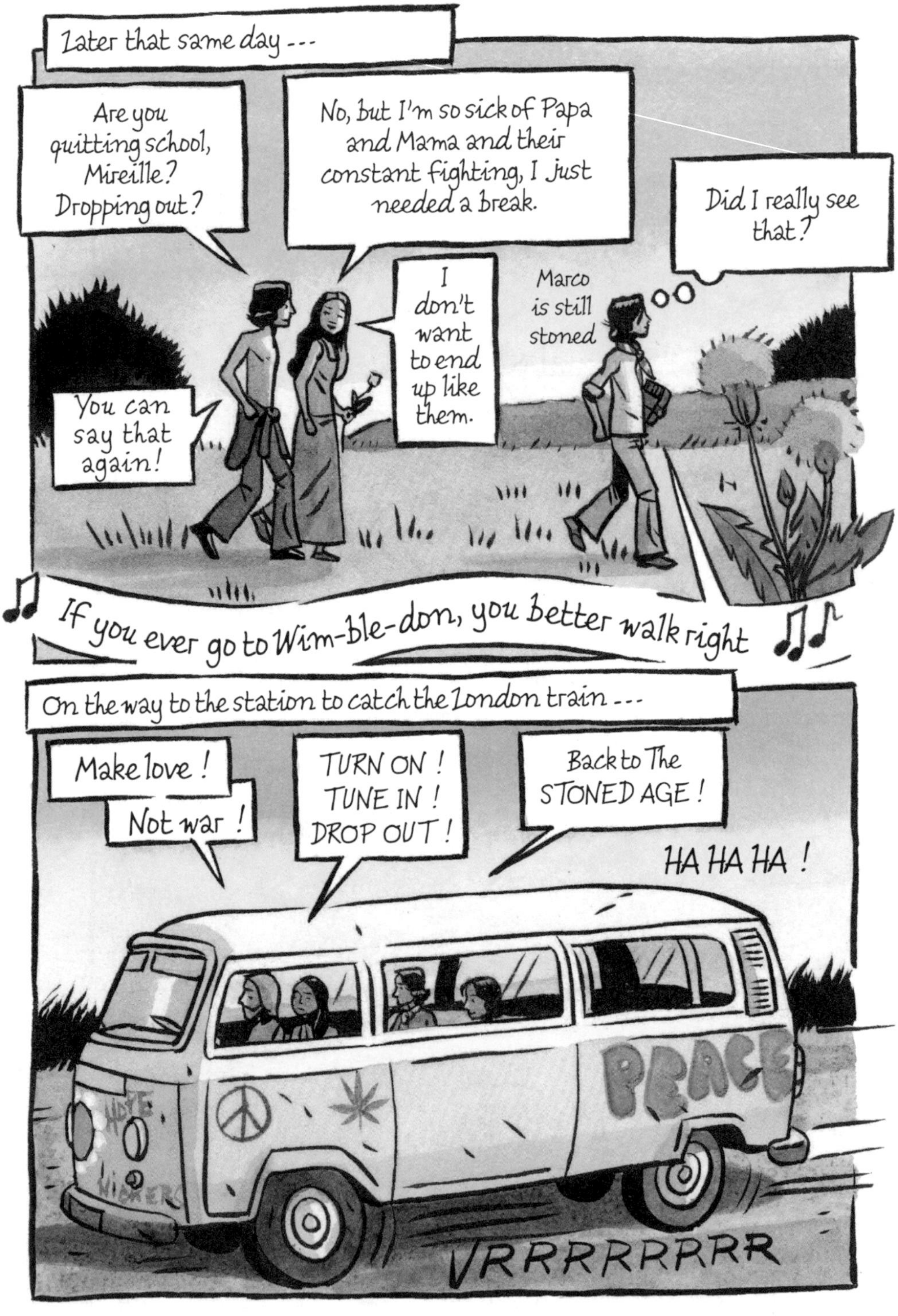
Later that same day ...
Are you quitting school, Mireille? Dropping out?
No, but I'm so sick of Papa and Mama and their constant fighting, I just needed a break.
Did I really see that?
I don't want to end up like them.
Marco is still stoned
You can say that again!
If you ever go to Wim-ble-don, you better walk right
On the way to the station to catch the London train ...
Make love!
Not war!
TURN ON! TUNE IN! DROP OUT!
Back to The STONED AGE!
HA HA HA!
PEACE
VRRRRRRRR

ON THE ROAD AGAIN

In 1972, Dominique dropped out of the Lycée and hit the road ---

Citroën
sheep-truck

Bêêê
Bêêê

Bêêê

Bêêê

Where you going?

Uh --- How about Katmandu?

?!

I'll drop you at the next town – that OK?!

OK !!!

Our parents were devastated.

Khánh, I'm worried sick!!

Yvette, it's time for him to be responsible. He's 19!

But he's your son, for God's sake!!

You always belittled him because he's not like you! Because he's not an INTELLECTUAL!

Not at all! But he needs an education or he needs to find a job!

It was no fun being under the same roof as Papa and Mama, both upset and ready to explode because of Domi leaving home.. And with Mireille at Durham --- Luckily I had my little sister Anh-Noëlle.

Mama blames everything on Papa and calls him a MANDARIN!

Domi was always a mystery to me.

She's says it's Papa's fault that Domi left!

As soon as he got his French passport,* he split. Before, with the Vietnamese passport, he couldn't.

It's not fair.

SNIF SNIF

Domi has to come home! A whole month and not a word!

He just doesn't care about us, that's all!

Yeah! He's selfish. And Papa called the police!

* At age 18, we Truong children opted for French citizenship. Legally, Domi and I could have been drafted into the Saigon army at 16.

189

Before Dominique embarked on his long disappearance (from December 1971 to April 1972), we shared a room on the third floor of our house in Wimbledon. Here's what Domi wrote in a letter to our sister Mireille:

> I'm listening to the Sunday Hit Parade on Radio One* Marco is ironing his pants for tomorrow.
>
> SCRATCH SCRATCH

Room I shared with Domi at 6C Grosvenor Hill Rd., Wimbledon

> I have a psychadelic view of the street and beyond from my desk. I'm listening to the records Marco borrowed. On Friday, I passed my math test. I try to work during the week-end but it's hard because sometimes you just feel like going to the Common, or watching TV, in other words, doing nothing...

*Radio 1 was a rock station launched by the BBC at the end of 1967

Of the few works of art Dominique left us, here is an undated and unsigned gouache I saw him paint at the end of 1971, before he ran away. It's the "psychedelic view" from our window.

In a letter to her parents from October 12, 1971, Mama wrote: "Dominique wrote a four-page paper on Rimbaud on Sunday, and his father shook his head in amazement at the well constructed sentences, linked by excellent transitions ---" And in a letter from December 9, 1971, Mama

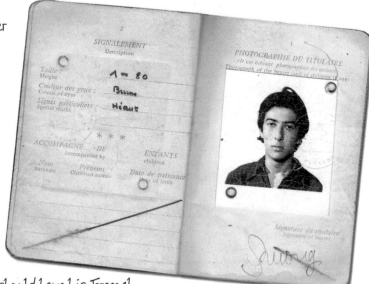

added: "Dominique should have his French passport soon and with no problem. He falls asleep with his head on a political economy textbook, or on Albert Camus' The Plague."

Mama *didn't* write a single letter between December 1971 and April 1972 — the period when Domi was gone. Maybe she preferred to talk to her parents on the phone.

What *did* he do during those four months?

"Truong" is a Vietnamese name isn't it?

Yeah, yeah!

That's what I thought. I fought in Indochina!

V-R-RRRR

Domi *did* what a lot of young people had done: he HIT THE ROAD!

I couldn't stay with my parents anymore.

Me neither!

He met girls --- He partied ---

We heard nothing from Domi until he made a friend, and that friend's mother called us, four months after he left. He didn't make it to Katmandu. He got as far as Nice---

He PANHANDLED --- or SLEPT OUTSIDE ---

He experienced LONELINESS too --- So finally, Domi came home.

Dominque's return was not easy ---

I don't want to go back to school!

I'm not going to do my Lower Sixth Form three times over!

SIGH!

Our former closeness was gone. Dominique tuned me out. He spent hours drawing, or just sleeping.

There! Dominique decided to quit his studies, but he can't just do nothing now!

Let him recuperate, Khánh! He was as thin as a rail when he came back.

Why don't you take a Valium?

Dominique took back his spot in the room we shared. He had changed since his disappearance, but said nothing about it. Not a word. His mind was elsewhere. I remember seeing him paint flowers in gouache - - -

His painting impressed me. I drew too, but I would never have dared to give such transparency to those spear-shaped leaves.

Dominique ended up trying his hand at door-to-door sales, hoping to pawn off sets of "Encyclopedia Britannica" in the working-class suburbs of London.

That didn't last long, since the market was saturated. Next, Domi found a job in a clothing store in the center of London, SHUBETTE, on Great Portland Street. He was a packer, preparing shipments for mail-order sales. One day he got caught coming back from work without a ticket.

In a desperate-sounding letter from August 1972, he confided his feelings to Mireille, who had left her hippy commune and taken up her studies again.

> Dear Mireille,
> I'm depressed. I got caught without a ticket on the way home from work. That's the second time. I didn't say I was coming from Great Portland Street, despite the threats. I don't know what I'm going to say or do. I don't feel like eating or sleeping.   Love, Dominique
> P.S.: I think I'd go to jail if it weren't for Papa and Mama. I could pay off the fine that way and I'd appreciate my life and freedom more after it was over.

A sad letter! Still, our brother Dominique had a plan ---

Mama, I'm going to work really hard for three years ---
I'LL SAVE UP! And afterward, I'LL OPEN AN ART SUPPLY STORE!

Oh? Is that so ---? Well --- it's worth taking a chance, right?

The tension was rising between Papa and Dominique. And it was rubbing off on my parents.

The clash was inevitable. I don't remember what set it off. I only remember the result.

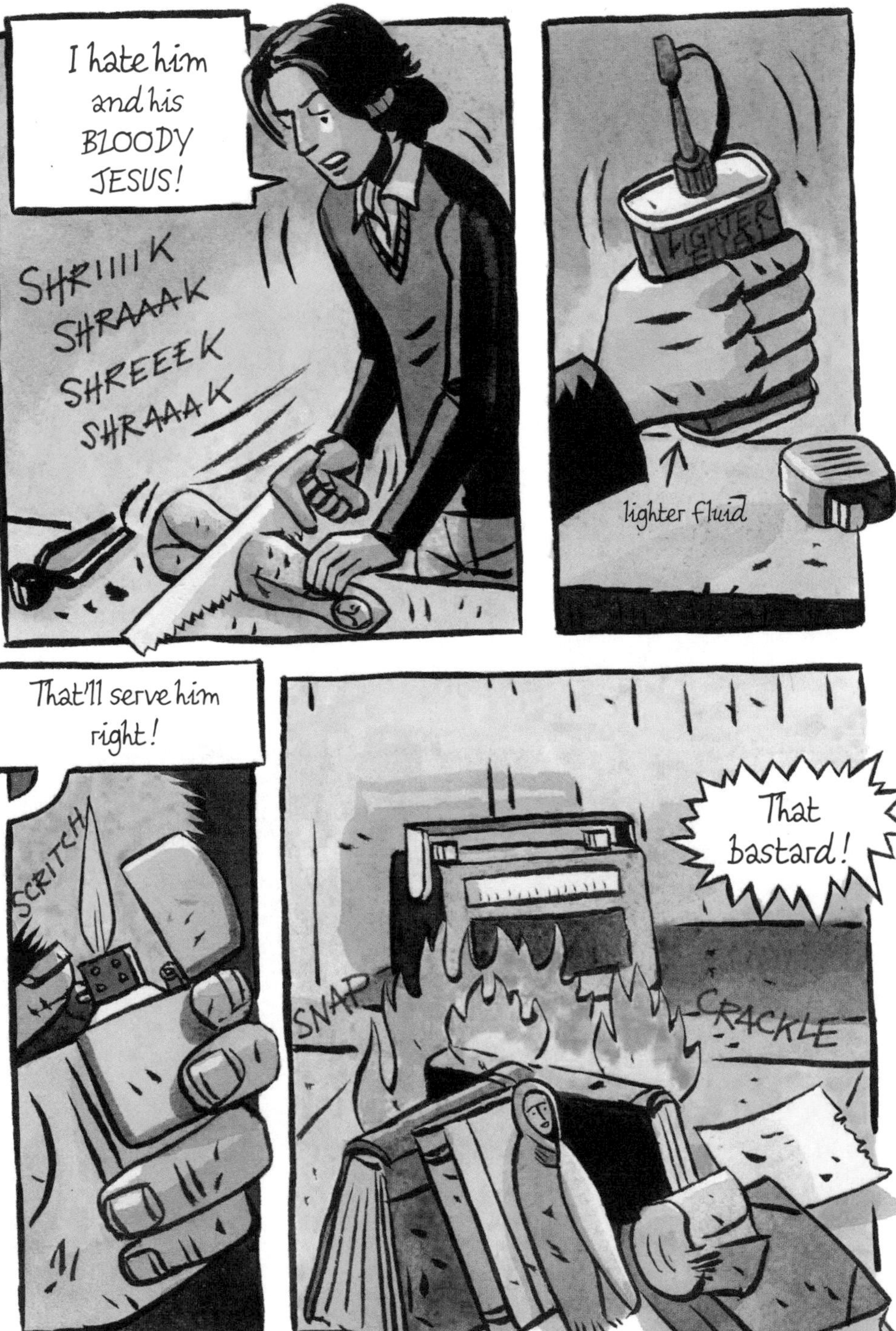
I hate him and his BLOODY JESUS!
SHRIIIIK
SHRAAAK
SHREEEK
SHRAAAK
lighter fluid
That'll serve him right!
SCRITCH
That bastard!
SNAP
CRACKLE

It was a shame that our parents didn't encourage Dominique to develop his artistic talents. Mama had sensed them. His project to open an art supply store was a sign. But Domi wasn't sufficiently aware of his talents either. When I look at this third gouache – neither dated nor signed – it's clear he should have gone into the arts.

I can recognize the Sillon beach in Saint-Malo. Our Saint-Malo Grandpa, wearing a beret and gray suit, is putting up the beach tent. One of the tall slender girls lying on the sand could be Mireille. And is the heavy-headed thinker leaning on the breakwater Dominique Ai My (his Vietnamese name means "he who loves beauty")?

Shortly after his funeral pyre of Papa's favorite objects, my brother took a room in the city, close to the French Lycée.

Letter dated
November 30, 1972

Dear Mireille,
    I found a room on Queensbury Place, the street next to the Lycée. Nine pounds a week. If you want, you can invite your friends. Try to find someone who knows how to paint.   Your brother Dominique
P.S.: Try and bring back lots of "goodie" from Durham, I'll pay you back.

"Goodies," of course, was secret code for cannabis. After Domi rejected his father's Christian god, he began a quest for a new faith and a new community. Like many hippies, he turned to Indian religions.

BEACH RED

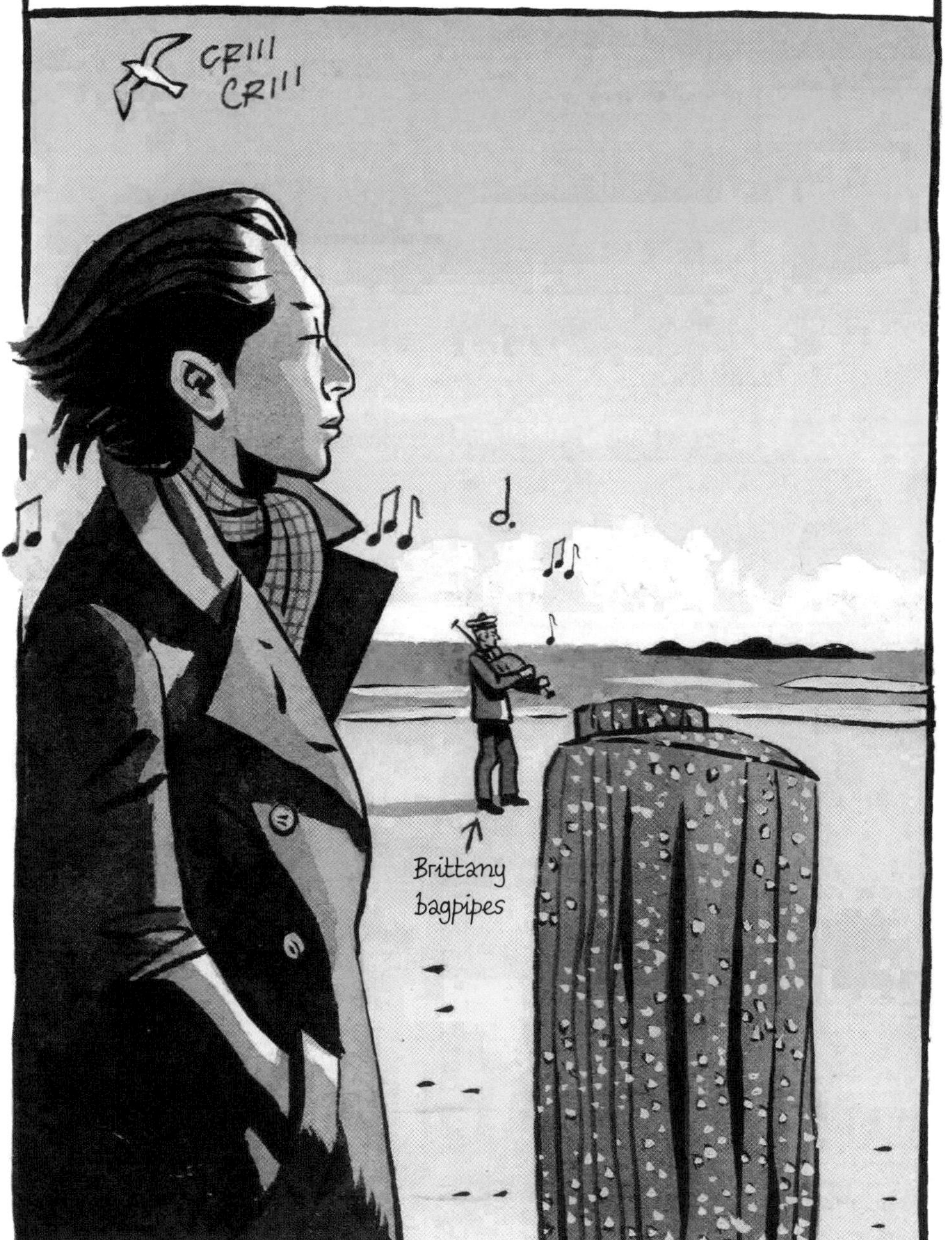
CRIII
CRIII
Brittany bagpipes
Breakwater

July 1972. On vacation at our maternal grandparents' place in Brittany, my mother was still in crisis mode, and suddenly decreed I would do my last two years of lycée at boarding school in Saint-Malo, at the Lycée Jacques-Cartier. Quite the change after London!

Grand Bé

Fort national

The French Lycée in London has had a very bad influence on you, Marco.

!?

Shit! I'm going to lose all my friends!

But my mother's decision wasn't all that bad. I was glad to put some distance between me and our house in Wimbledon, where life wasn't very rosy, and the tensions were high.

We're absolutely delighted to have you with us, Marco!

Me too, Grandpa! I'll be happy staying with you.

I got along well with my grandparents, and I had a friend from the French Lycée in London, Bernard C., whose parents had taken over the Hôtel de l'Univers on the place Chateaubriand, inside the city walls.

'ello mate!

Are the natives friendly? Is the hunting any good?

HA HA HA!

Nice to see you, mate! Long time no see!

HÔTEL DE L'UNIVERS

Bernard and I were the same age. He worked full-time at the hotel during the summer season to help his parents. He asked me if I wanted to share the job with him. I took up his offer right away.

washing station, hotel kitchen

You'll see, there are different things to do, you won't just be washing dishes. We work with the pastry, we help out with the bar, things like that ---

Okay, that's great!

I learned a lot at the Hôtel de l'Univers. Bernard's father was a top-level chef, and he'd been working in kitchens since he was 12. He had a lofty idea of manual labor.

Try to look sharp when you're working!

Stand up straight on your two feet!

It's safer that way. The kitchen is a dangerous place.

Bon Secours Swimming Pool

My grandparents --- Saint-Malo --- the Hôtel de l'Univers --- the sea ---

Bernard's mother worked the front desk and managed the books. She seemed like a level-headed woman, what Mama could have been if she weren't sick.

HA HA HA! You and Bernard are a couple of twins!

EEEEK
EEEK

YAHOO!

Come on, let's go swimming!

The beach --- No more arguments at home --- Now that's the life!

The latest news from Vietnam cast a shadow over this carefree life. In April 1972, Hanoi launched its spring-summer offensive. This time, 200,000 North Vietnamese regulars pushed their way into the South, backed by hundreds of tanks, on three fronts: south of the 17th parallel at Quang Tri, in the central highlands of Kontum, and to the south, only 30 kilometers from Saigon. This was the hardest blow struck against the South since Têt in 1968.

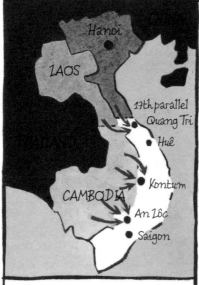

North Vietnamese Nguyên Huê offensive, April-October 1972

ROOAAAR

Sapper

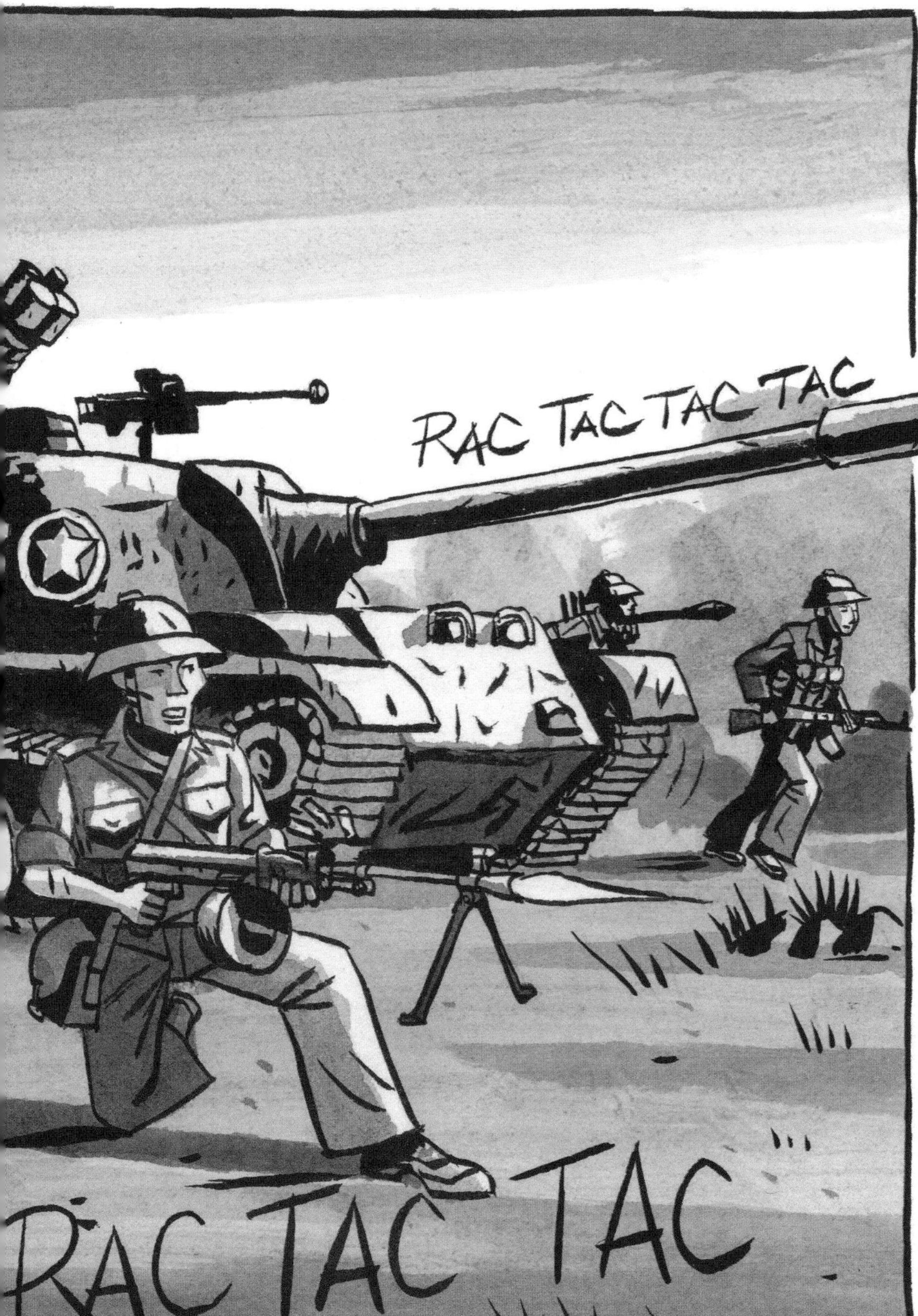
RAC TAC TAC TAC
RAC TAC TAC...

Wanting to reinforce its positions in the Paris peace talks that were going nowhere, Hanoi dropped its usual guerrilla tactics and used a Soviet-style, full frontal armored assault. Peking and Moscow supplied the heavy artillery, and young Vietnamese were the cannon fodder. With this blitzkrieg, the Communists hoped to rout the soldiers of Saigon; Uncle Sam had been transferring responsibility for the war to them over the last three years.

It was true: traumatized by the 1968 Têt Offensive, America was looking for a way out. Nixon had promised to bring the boys home. The South Vietnamese would have to make it on their own. As the French followed the Tour de France bicycle race, I was wondering whether the South Vietnamese soldiers would hold the fort.

* Bô dôi: North Vietnamese regulars

THEY DID HOLD THE FORT: the 200,000 men sent by Hanoi felt the power of the South's ferocious resistance. Quang Tri in the north, Kontum in the center, and An Lôc, a two-hour drive from Saigon, were overrun, then taken back. American air power made a contribution, but battles were won on the ground. Quang Tri, Kontum, and An Lôc were brilliant victories.

Stamps from the South celebrating the victory

The losses from the 1972 offensive were enormous. There were 25,000 civilian and military casualties in the South. The North Vietnamese lost 100,000 men. Three hundred Americans also died in the battle.

*Victory

During our afternoon break from work, I would go to the beach and try to follow the military ups and down of the "Summer of Flames," 1972, with a group of Bernard's friends.

sailor's caps →

sailor's sweater

striped → version

Come on, we're going to down a few pints!

NEIL YOUNG

501 jeans →

CLING CLING

Brittany sweater

← short sailing boots

tiger-striped jacket worn by South Vietnamese elite units →

Oh, yeah? The shit's hit the fan over there?

← condom belt

What? You haven't heard?

WE TOOK BACK QUANG TRI FROM THE NORTH!

Sometimes in the group, there was a Vietnamese guy – no doubt the only one in Saint-Malo – who stuck out because of his look. The would-be tough guys of Saigon – called "cowboys" – wore the same clothes.

* Lực, my Vietnamese first name, means "strength."
*Hùng means "hero."
* Victory! Victory!

213

When school started up again in September 1972, I bought a used scooter with the money I made at the Hôtel de l'Univers. It was great, zipping around Saint-Malo! I discovered middle-of-the-road French pop. Quite a shock!

veteran of Algeria

Non, je ne regrette rien

paratrooper cap

♪♫ Laisse-moi vivre ma vie

the Môle beach

worms

At age 15, I was already reading up on the history of Vietnam. My father had every book on the subject. He lent me the Hô Chi Minh biography by Jean Lacouture – very favorable to Uncle Hô – and many other books from all points of view. He thought we should hear different opinions in order to form our own.

In my room in Saint-Malo

Hô Chi Minh poster →

Avec LECLERC en Indo

corsaires de Saint-Malo

Bigea...

*"Laisse-moi vivre ma vie" (Let Me Live My Life), Frédéric François, 1972.

Je ne veux plus être celui qui ne connaît que les chagrins. ♪♪

Syrupy music!

Help me!

Dinan wharf

old sailor's slicker →

I'M GONNA CRY!

the "Mobylette," Motobécane AV 34, 1966

In '72, only ten years after the war in Algeria, stories were coming out. Films were being produced. I paid attention; I knew those camo uniforms.

Look at that! Our soldiers in Saigon had the same outfits.

Here, we're the fascists, and Uncle Hô is the hero!

In France under President Georges Pompidou (who came in after the uproar of May '68), the right had been in power for 14 years. Young people there could choose between four "types." Of course, like in any game of musical chairs, you could stay as one type for a while, then move on by changing your look.

The Silent Majority

the "Baba Cools" *

Only young French people into politics were interested in the Vietnam War. The hippies were into pacifism. I had met the "Peace and Love" gang in England, so it was nothing new on this side of the Channel ---

*Take care !
*Hippies

There weren't many young people in Saint-Malo in 1972 who would claim to be on the right, and even fewer on the far right. I only met one who was a monarchist. The ones who had something to say about the war in what was called Indochina (Vietnam, Laos, Cambodia) were leftists. And only a few of them bothered to talk about it.

For them, things were simple. The Vietnam War was a lopsided conflict with, on one side, the humble David (North Vietnam, the NLF in the South) against the American Goliath. Of course, they sided with the weak against the strong. They thought the South Vietnamese who were against Communism were mere "puppets," a non-existent, phantom nation ---

In September, I started at Jacques Cartier Lycée.

Hi! You new here? Where you from?

Hi! I'm Vietnamese, but my mother's from Saint-Malo. And I lived in London --- What's your name?

Soazig!

The two sports we had to do in gym were weightlifting and rugby. Mr. Gardy wanted to improve our physique.

HA HA HA   HA HA HA

CLING

I discovered team sports in Saint-Malo, thanks to my friend Bernard. He was the captain of the first-year rugby team, and I joined. That way I improved my collection of rugby songs.

♪♪ Le curé de Camaret* a les couilles qui pendent.

* "The priest of Camaret's balls hang low---" Camaret-sur-Mer is a town on the Brittany coast.

TRUONG! I feel sorry for the woman who'll end up in your bed!

Mr. Gardy said the same thing to all the boys. Here is the apex of Olympic weightlifting: the SNATCH!

1. ARGHH — The starting position

2. HMPF! — The extension position

3. PUFF PUFF — The receiving position

4. PHEW! — The standing position

The boarding school had boys and girls from the surrounding countryside. I would keep them amused with my sketches of the headmaster, who was from Alsace.

WE HAF VAYS OF MAKING YOU TALK!!

SCRATCH

SCRATCH

One of the boarding school staff members belonged to the French Communist Party. Michel was a good guy, but his ready-made opinions about the Vietnam War rang like Orwellian Newspeak to me.

Progressive forces around the world support the Vietnamese people in their struggle for peace against American imperialism and its lackeys!

The Vietnamese people, in the North and the South, want peace. But the Communists in Hanoi love peace so much they just invaded the South with their entire army and hundreds of tanks.

You know what the lackeys of the American paper tigers would tell you?

GO JUMP IN THE VOLGA!

The Communists don't represent the Vietnamese people as a whole.

You never set foot in Vietnam! All you know is what you read in your Party Bible!

Ha ha! Little reactionary!

In 1972, the French Communist Party, with Georges Marchais as its head, won 20% of the vote.

Michel's credo, simplistic as it was, at least was altruistic. He thought he was going to liberate the Vietnamese. But often I heard a more strident note from those who were nostalgic for France's former colonial domination.

Sometimes I helped out at the hotel bar ---

Hey, are you a little Viet, maybe?

I used to live there. In Saigon! Those were good days!

Yeah, a little half-breed! I figured as much--- I can spot them.

My father is Vietnamese ---

And the girls back there! Docile little dolls, the way we like them! Mmm!

And boys too, for the guys that like that! HA HA HA!

It takes all kinds, huh? True, or not? HA HA HA!

Besides, back there, it's not always easy to tell them apart from the girls! HA HA HA!

The guy hung out at the bar --- Whenever he left a tip, he'd say, "Now you can open a laundry!"

At the Saint-Malo Lycée, there was a French teacher who taught secretarial classes. We'll call her Yolande. She was good-hearted and dedicated to her students. And she was a Maoist. Mao was her god.

Here, Yolande, I brought you some Chinese posters from London!

classroom →

sweater Grandma knitted →

Oh, thank you! I love those pictures.

I bought the propaganda posters in Soho,* when I was visiting my parents. In 1972, in France, Mao was clothed in a magical aura. Many progressives, disappointed by the revelations of Stalin's crimes, cast their hopes on Chinese-style Communism. Maybe they thought it was more agrarian, innocent, bucolic, and exotic?

WONDERFUL!

Look at the Great Helmsman, he looks so gentle and sweet!!

!?

* Location of London's Chinatown, and home to a Chinese bookstore that sold Maoist propaganda for a song.

When I heard that, I realized that the South Vietnamese cause – with its hopes of avoiding life in a totalitarian system – had little chance of being understood in the West.

I enjoyed the calm atmosphere of my grandparents' house. Sometimes we wondered about Mama's bipolar disorder. What could have caused her anxiety and torment?

Your mother was very afraid when we had to evacuate Saint-Malo in August of '44

With good reason!

Your Grandpa found us a barn to stay in.

TAC

The Germans received orders: they were to fight to the last man. They forced us civilians to evacuate the city.

TIC TAC TIC TAC TIC

Your grandfather was the first to leave with your Aunt Annie. They took the road to Rennes in search of shelter.

I was with your mother Yvette. We joined the crowds fleeing Saint-Malo, which was burning.

TIC TAC TIC

I pushed Yvette into the ditch and threw myself on her ---

The Americans had started bombing ---

SHE WAS TERRIFIED!

We were out in the countryside. The Germans trying to reach their exterior defensive position mixed in with us ---

She really thought she was going to die ---

Two Allied fighters bombed and strafed our group.

Maybe something inside her broke that day ---

Meanwhile, the Paris peace talks had been dragging on for four years. The three sides wouldn't budge an inch.

Lê Đức Thọ (North Vietnam)

The longer the talks go on, the better it is for us!

Uncle Sam must pull his troops out of the South! The Saigon puppet regime will flee! Vietnam will be reunified under Uncle Hô's banner!

Henry Kissinger (USA)

Let's get the US out of this mess, and save face!

Hanoi must recall the 250,000 men it has in the South, and elections will let the South Vietnamese choose the political system they want!

Nguyễn Văn Thiệu (South Vietnam)

The Americans are negotiating with Hanoi behind our backs!

The North must pull back behind their borders! They're just waiting for the GIs to leave, and they'll launch a new offensive!

It was a stalemate. To force the North Vietnamese to make concessions, President Nixon launched Operation Linebacker II, the most massive bombing campaign of the war.

Based on a Hugh Haynie cartoon in the Louisville Courier-Journal, 1972.

Joan Baez, the pacifist folksinger, was visiting an American prisoner of war camp in North Vietnam when the fire started raining down. She endured 60 raids over 12 days and nights of hell.

An album was born of this emotional experience: "Where Are You Now, My Son?" * (1973). It was partially recorded in Hanoi. "Where are you now, my son?" was the despairing cry of a Vietnamese mother searching for her child in the ruins.

I was in London during Nixon's Christmas bombing.

The December bombing pushed the North Vietnamese to return to the negotiating table, and a peace accord was finally signed January 27, 1973.

US, GO HOME! Too bad for the South!

A new era of peace is beginning.

Yes, and it will be a durable peace!

It's just a matter of time. We will never stop fighting for the reunification of Vietnam!

In Saigon, President Thiêu had to accept the accord that let his main supporter withdraw without losing face. But he was deeply bitter. The South was being undermined.

With the GIs gone and an army of 250,000 in the South, the Communists must be celebrating!

Peace is an illusion. Hanoi will never cease its campaign to take over the South.

The wolves are in the sheepfold!

Carefully preserving his image, Lê Duc Tho made reassuring promises.

Reunification will be a peaceful, step-by-step process! *

* January 24, 1973 declaration in Paris.

A strange sort of peace settled in. In South Vietnam, people could move around freely again, more or less.

Much later, my friend Tin — who had written me back in 1965 — told me a story from 1973. As they approached a VC-controlled zone, his mother was so afraid he'd be kidnapped by the guerrillas that she made him wear a wig!

I wouldn't have minded seeing that!

* God in heaven!

In the spring of 1974, a few weeks before final exams, a young French guy who had lived in Cambodia showed up at our lycée.

I was in my final year at Lycée Descartes in Phnom Penh...

The Khmer Rouge Katyusha rockets rained down night and day, they didn't care where!

Here in France, you know the progressives support the Khmer Rouge?!

I know! My parents read "Le Monde."

They're teachers. They sent me here to be safe. I hope they'll get out if the Khmer Rouge take the capital!

I don't know what happened to that boy and his parents after the fall of Phnom Penh on April 17, 1975.

The next day in "Le Monde," a story ran, written by Jacques Decornoy, dateline Phnom Penh. "Cambodia will be democratic, and all rights will be respected," the journalist wrote.

I remember the shock when the 1973 coup in Chile was announced. The brutal repression orchestrated by General Pinochet showed just how far Washington was willing to go to snuff out emerging Marxist regimes in its backyard, South America.

In August 1974, the Watergate scandal forced Nixon to resign. We know now that Hanoi was waiting for him to fall to make its move in South Vietnam. I paid vague attention to the news, more concerned with final exams and girls than "Tricky Dick."

AUTUMN IN PARIS

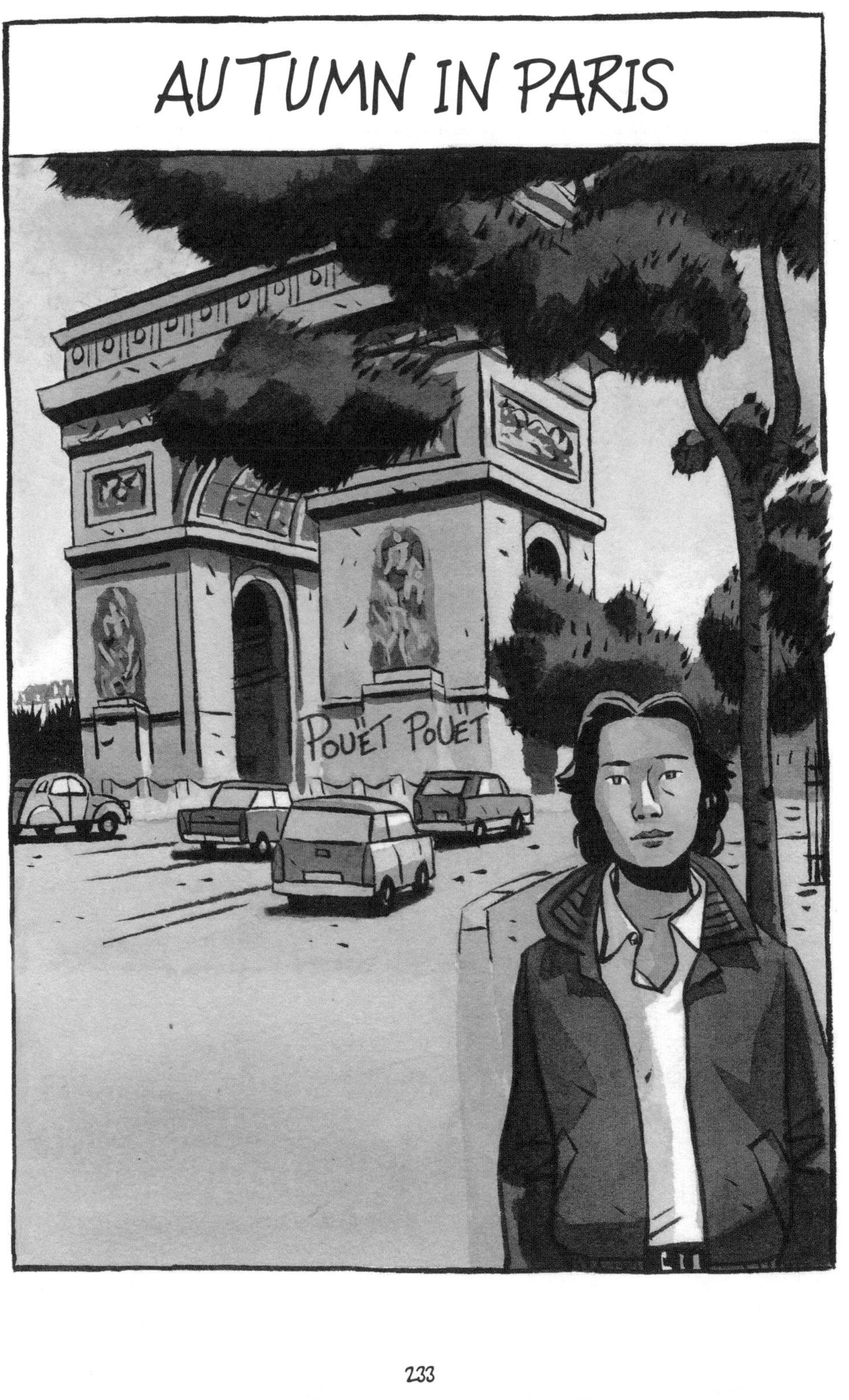
POUËT POUËT

In September 1974, I began my studies at the famed Sciences Po in Paris, following in the footsteps of my father, who earned his degree there in 1951. The upscale, socially conservative students with their preppie look were exotic to me. Valéry Giscard d'Estaing had just been elected president of France, and his son Henri was in first year at Sciences Po. Princess Caroline of Monaco attended too.

Arnys shirt

club tie

Church on Sunday, Alix?

cashmere turtleneck

Yes, Henri, I sing in the choir.

Raglan sleeve raincoat, Burberry's, putty-colored (not too new!)

"Le Monde" (a tradition)

Old England gloves

Céline handbag

Loden coat

Scotch House skirt from London

Burlington socks

3-cm cuffs!

Church's or Weston's

Céline shoes with bridle-bit buckles

Classic but elegant, these children of the French bourgeoisie seemed old before their time. Had they ever challenged the status quo? I doubted it.

I remember a Cambodian I'd met at the student restaurant.

Join us! The FUNK* and the comrades from the Laotian and Vietnamese guerrillas will triumph!

Even the King of Cambodia, Sihanouk, is with us!

Nothing but talk...

I know that.

* The "Front uni national du Kampuchea," or Khmer Rouge

Norodom Sihanouk renounced his throne. With Red China behind him, he took over the FUNK leadership!

Did he renounce polygamy too? They say he has seven wives. "Monogamy equals monotony," so he says!

- HA HA HA HA !

I wonder if my friend the militant went back to his country after 1975. If he did, he was surely liquidated by the Khmer Rouge. They hated anyone contaminated by the West.

Even Prince Sihanouk, harried from his throne by a military putsch backed by the United States, was with the Khmer Rouge! That's just how confused things were in those days.

All the Sciences Po students who are cool are for the Viêt-Cong and the Hanoi regime!

This movie isn't going to change their minds, on the contrary!!

It's all very convenient. T[he] film is an inventory of th[e] atrocities committed by th[e] Americans in Vietnam --

We South Vietnamese simply don't exist!

The doc forgets one fundamental truth: the Hanoi regime is a Big Brother totalitarian system!

Actually, only right-wing students distrusted the Stalinist, Maoist regime in Hanoi. Either it was a knee-jerk reflex, or the result of the experience of their elders. There were far-right students at Sciences Po, and they reminded me of the skinheads in London – just more bourgeois. They believed in the superiority of the white race, and had a tradition of anti-Semitism --- For them, the Vietnamese were noble savages always ready to revert to their slanty-eyed ways ---

Con-treuh les Viêts ♩. Con-treuh ♫.

* "Against the Viets," a paratrooper marching song of the French Indochina war.

Mixed in with the anti-Communism of far-right student factions was a certain nostalgia for the France's former empire and its finest pearl, Indochina. For that reason, France's support of the South seemed founded on dubious premises. Their posters and emblems echoed other goose-stepping totalitarian systems.

You must submit!

NO!

Most Sciences Po students kept their opinion about the Vietnam War to themselves, but on the left, the socialists, Communists, and radicals created a common front, guided by the same slogans: anti-colonialism and Third Worldism. They all wanted Friday to free himself from Robinson. But just a minute – they were out to run Robinson out of town, but what system did they want for Friday?

"Ecrasons les valets du Vietcong!": "Crush the Viêt-cong lackeys!"

Eager to save us, the left applauded the armed movements that promised to deliver the last of the colonized, those "wretched of the earth." Posters with lyrical slogans called on people to wholeheartedly support tendencies about which the militants in 1974 knew very little. It didn't matter that these guerrillas were backed by the Soviet bloc, since at the time, Communism still had its allure.

In July 1974, the publication of The Gulag Archipelago, a book by the former political prisoner Aleksandr Solzhenitsyn about a Soviet forced hard labor camp, should have alerted those enamored with Hanoi as to Communism's true nature. But the idea of an anti-capitalist, egalitarian revolution was too romantic to resist. As for the South Vietnamese who rejected the Communist system, the left chose to believe they simply didn't exist. The efforts of Uncle Sam's puppets didn't count for anything.

In my room in the attic, under the eaves at 3 rue des Renaudes in Paris's 17th arrondissement, I had a close neighbor. The sweet music of female ecstasy was a constant accompaniment as I tried to master the ins and outs of the French political system.

♪ Oh, oui, oui! ... Encore! ... Oui, c'est bon!... Oui, prends-moi! ... Plus vite! ... ♪

Article 493: The Prime Minister, after due deliberation with the Council of Ministers, will take responsibility before the National Assembly ---

Shit! Some guys have all the fun!

Aaaaah Ouiiiii! Encooore! Plus foooort!

Georges Vedel's course on the Constitution of the Fifth Republic

One day, hearing someone knock on my neighbor's door, I pretended that the person had knocked on mine. I was curious to see the lucky lady who was visiting the 6th-floor Don Juan.

♪ Oh, baby, you love me so right

Oh, pardon me! I thought it was for me.

Saint-Malo sailor's sweater

My neighbor in his attic room looked like a Julio Iglesias-style Latin lover. One day, his door was half open, and I peeked inside. His love nest was completely covered with centerfolds from skin mags. Very chic!

linoleum

A few paragraphs of Jean-Claude Casanova's course on economy later ---

Love me baby

TOC TOC

Aaaah!

OUIIIIII!!

C'est booon!

I've come to see Monsieur Haddad.

--- The European SNAKE IN THE TUNNEL (!) is a tool for limiting the --- the --- fluctuation in currency values within the member states of the EEC ---

While I was sweating it out in Sciences Po, in the heart of the French establishment, my brother Domi was in Iran, on the way back from Katmandu.

After his French military service in the Air Force Security Detail, Domi, age 21, hitchhiked to Nepal. At the end of 1974, he wrote to Mireille, who was married and living in Nottingham.

At the Saudi Arabian embassy, I really freaked out the military attaché! I must've looked a mess. I'd smoked up the night before and there was lots of oil mixed in with the hasch, which had a strange effect on me. The attaché sent me packing...

Get out of here!

WHIIIIIIR

* How much?

Iran was but a stop on Domi's long solitary drifting journey that would end five years later. While traveling in India, Dominique found refuge in an ashram in Pune, in the state of Maharashtra.

An ashram is a retreat presided over by a guru. Westerners were flooding into Pune's meditation center to encounter its spiritual master, Bhagwan Shree Rajneesh.

Call me Swami Ramamurti!

Dominique became a disciple - a "sannyasin" - of the Pune community. He changed his identity and his appearance, dressed in orange and brown, and always wore a large necklace of wooden pearls decorated with a medallion featuring his new master's face.

He seemed to have found a new family there, all fascinated and in awe of Guru Rajneesh.

Neither thought nor mind nor choice - keep the silence, be rooted in yourselves ---

Forget everything you have learned up until now!

Guru Rajneesh - a genius to some, a crook to others - died in 1990. His cult lives on under the name Osho.

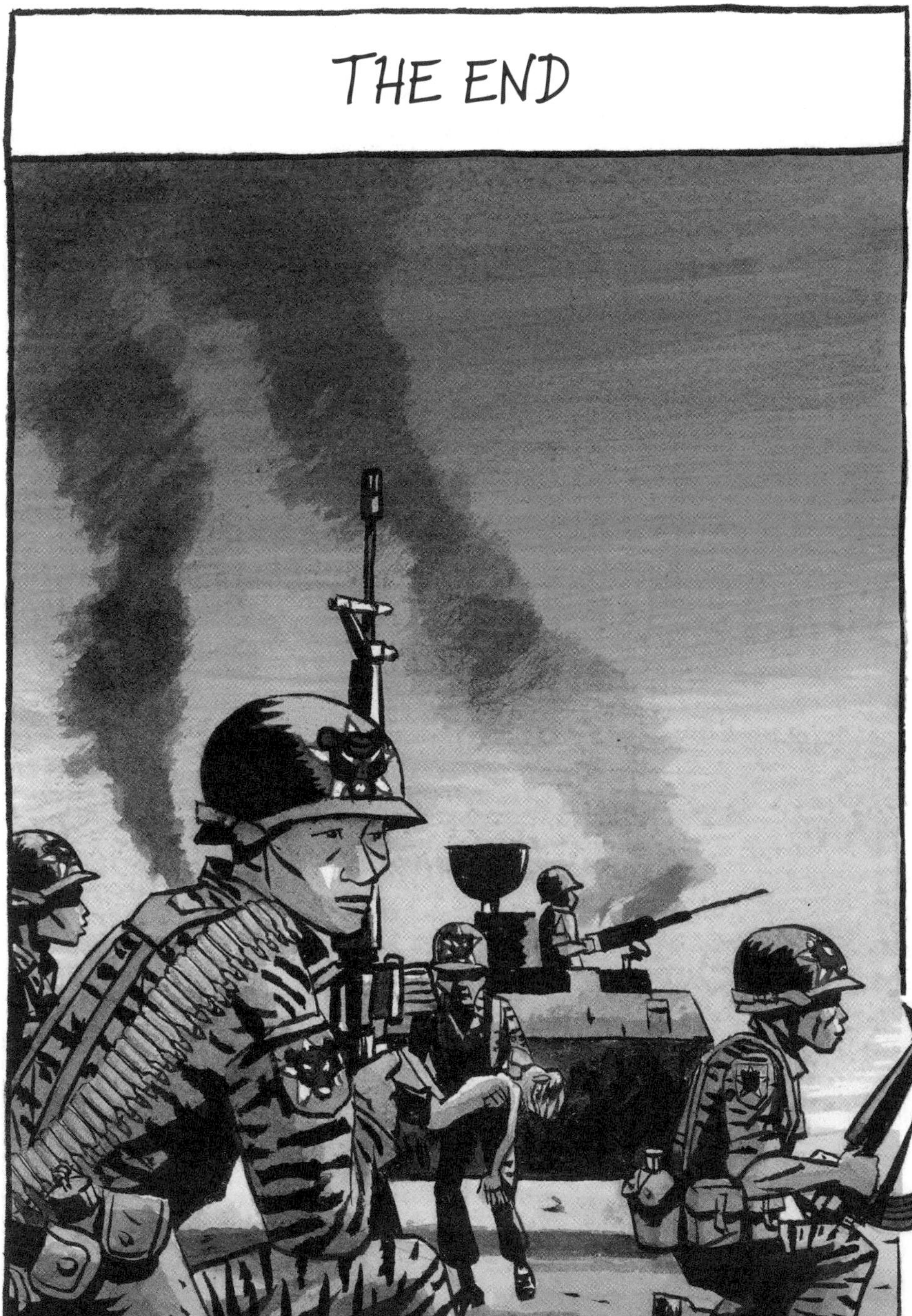
THE END

In December 1974, in violation of the 1973 peace agreement, Hanoi sent two divisions into the province of Phuoc Long, a strategic point in South Vietnam.

Mister President, Hanoi is out to test our determination to support our South Vietnamese allies!

I know!

But our B-52s will stay on their runways. The American people are sick of hearing about Vietnam.

Gerald Ford, Nixon's successor

AMERICA WANTS OUT!

In January 1975, in the absence of American air strikes – the usual reprisals – North Vietnam prepared its full-scale offensive for the spring of 1975 which, against all expectations, resulted in the collapse of the South.

Ford is not made of the same stuff as Nixon. Let's advance before the monsoon!

The battle will last another two years, but we will prevail!

Have patience! The final victory is near. LIBERATE THE SOUTH!

Two years after the 1973 cease-fire, largely ignored by both sides, the Vietnamese people were weary of endless warfare.

In the North, there were shortages of everything except weaponry supplied by the "brotherhood" of the Soviet bloc.

In the South, the scarcity was less severe, but ammunition was rationed and spare parts had stopped coming because the US Congress didn't want to foot the bill ---

* "Twenty years of civil war and all a Vietnamese mother can bequeath her child is sorrow."
Gia tài của mẹ, Trịnh Công Sơn, 1965.

Early March 1975, and the Communist offensive began with a body blow to the South. Saigon's forces in the central highlands were routed.

RAC TAC TAC TAC TAC

Sadly, in their panic, 400,000 civilians from the central regions took to the roads, fleeing south in fear. Among them were the families of soldiers stationed in the zone. Any sort of orderly retreat became impossible. Many men from the South's army left their units to defend their families.

Figuring he could bring together his forces further south, President Thiêu of South Vietnam ordered the evacuation of the outposts in the central region.

Let's regroup around Saigon and the delta!

President Thiêu

It was a terrible *debacle*! Caught between cannon fire from the North and aerial attacks from the South in support of its ground troops, the refugees were cut to shreds. Of this "Convoy of Tears," only some 100,000 people made it safely to the south.

HOINK HOINK !

I followed the events from Paris with consternation.

QUANG TRI !

HUÊ !

DANANG ! Incredible !

"The major strong points in the center have collapsed, one after the other --- And now the South Vietnamese are facing frontal assaults from the People's Army at XUÂN LÔC, only 90 km from Saigon." SHIT !

At the end of March 1975, the North Vietnamese high command, sensing victory at hand, renamed its Spring Campaign No. 275 the "Hô Chi Minh Offensive."

May 19 would have been Uncle Hô's birthday!

Right ! He deserves a gift: that old whore Saigon!

HA ! HA ! HA ! HA !

Chicom rifle

250

On April 17, 1975, Phnom Penh, the capital of Cambodia, fell to the Khmer Rouge.

The next day, I scoured the papers. The right-wing dailies deplored the take-over of Phnom Penh. "Le Monde" cast a benevolent eye, while "Libération," with its Maoist tendencies, was triumphant.

* "On a blank sheet of paper free from any mark, the freshest and most beautiful characters can be written." Mao Zedong

Like many people in 1975, I wanted to believe that the coming of the Khmer Rouge would lead Cambodia on an independent, agrarian, egalitarian path --- But I had my doubts. The black-clad peasants reminded me of Viêt-Cong guerrillas.

WHICH ONE IS CHARLIE?

bush hat

Mao cap

black and white checked "krama" scarf

red and white checked "krama" scarf

black pajamas

black peasant pajamas

AK47

100-cartridge drum magazine

RPD light machine gun

Phnom Penh is only 250 km from Saigon, and the border zone - the Parrot's Beak - as early as 1945 became a sanctuary for units of the Viêt-Minh, and later the Viêt-Cong. In part, the Khmer Rouge were a creation of the South Vietnamese NLF and Hanoi, but the Chinese Maoist influence predominated among them. The Viêt-Cong and the Khmer Rouge inspired distrust and fear in me. Something about their look --- they were blood brothers.

In the days that followed, we learned that the 40,000 Khmer Rouge who entered Phnom Penh had emptied the city of its 2 million inhabitants, forcing them into the countryside. All their worldly goods – fridges, TVs, scooters, and everything else – were piled in the street and crushed to powder with steamrollers...

> I am the master now, and the West is no longer our tyrant!

That was only the beginning of the ordeal. The worst was yet to come.

In Vietnam, the situation was desperate. Only 62 km north of Saigon, the city of Xuân Lôc was attacked by 3 North Vietnamese divisions. It would fall on April 21, after 11 days of ferocious resistance.

> HẾT ĐẠN! HẾT ĐẠN!!*

RAC TAC TAC TAC

* Out of ammo!

Xuân Lôc was the last, great pitched battle of the war before the defense of Saigon. The 12,000 soldiers of the 18th Division commanded by General Lê Minh Dao fought 40,000 North Vietnam regulars for nine days. Though they knew the war was lost, the men of the 18th showed that South Vietnamese soldiers, so often denigrated, could match their enemies when it came to barbarity.

The North admitted that the battle had been "cruel." Its side suffered more than 5,000 casualties in the field, while the 18th Division of the South lost one man in three.

After the fall of Saigon, General Dao surrendered to the new masters on May 9, 1975. He spent 17 years in a reeducation camp before being freed. He now lives in the United States.

← Lê Minh Đảo

RAC TAC TAC TAC

BLAM

On April 21, Xuân Lôc fell, and the road to Saigon opened up to North Vietnamese troops. That same day, the president of the South, Nguyên Van Thiêu, gave a long televised speech deploring how the Americans had abandoned his country. Then he announced he was resigning.

Thiêu is deserting the sinking ship!

"The Best and the Brightest," David Halberstam, 1972

I just hope Saigon Grandpa and Grandma are safe! And all our family in Vietnam!

!

OPTALIX

President Thiêu has sought exile in Taiwan --- The winds of panic sweep through Saigon --- After the Huê massacres in 1968, the citizens of the capital fear a blood bath when the Communists conquer the city --- Hordes of armed looters are already at work ---

April 25, downstairs, at Café Le Diplomate.

C'est ma pri- èèè-èè- reuh Entends ma voâââ

Thanks!

Really?! The singer?! How come?

You hear? Mike Brant jumped off the balcony of his place on rue Erlanger. *

That day, I called my parents in London from the post office.

A little later ---

Good luck on your exams, Marco!

Marco, how are you?! Well, I managed to call my parents. They said they're staying no matter what happens and --- (silence) --- not to worry about them ---

Hi, MAMA! It's Marco.

I'll get your father. He knows what's happening in Vietnam!

We'll continue to follow the events, right, Marco?!

* Mike Brant, born Moishe Brand, was an Israeli singer and composer popular in France.

Despite his reserve, I could sense Papa's anxiety. Twenty years of war and hatred had him fearing the conqueror's revenge. Uncle Diên, one of Papa's brothers, had been Minister of Information in the Thiêu government. Our family had every reason to be afraid, knowing the fight was lost ---

On April 27, 1975, the enemy was at the gates. 100,000 North Vietnamese soldiers surrounded the capital. To add to the chaos, they fired Katyusha rockets randomly and indiscriminately. It felt like the end of the world.

On Tuesday, April 29, at 4 in the morning, the VC shelled the Saigon airport, cutting off any escape by plane.

US Ambassador Graham Martin held out as long as he could before admitting the situation was desperate. But in the end, he had to give the green light to Operation Frequent Wind, the largest helicopter evacuation in history. The signal to begin this aerial Dunkirk? A Bing Crosby tune.

In the Saigon suburbs, some units of the AR VN, the army of the South, put up stubborn resistance against the "liberators" from Hanoi. Hoàng Dan, a North Vietnam general, would later say, "If someone tells me we took Saigon without as much as breaking a light bulb, I'll hand him a shovel and make him dig graves for our dead!" On the Communist side, 6000 died during the battle of Saigon.

After the defeat, these soldiers were punished with long years of detention in reeducation camps. For the Communists, they were nothing but traitors.

Even today, more than 40 years after the end of the fighting, the current regime still calls them puppets and bandits, and American stooges

---

In the embassy offices, employees feverishly destroyed sensitive documents. In their haste, the workers forgot a file containing the names of 30,000 Vietnamese who had been very involved with the Americans. The file helped the conquerors eliminate their enemies after the fall of the South (according to Frank Snepp, formerly of the CIA).

Meanwhile, a panicked crowd rushed the gates of the United States embassy. In the chaos and madness, everyone tried to make it into the safe sanctuary.

On April 30, 1975, at 4:59 in the morning, US Ambassador Graham Martin finally stepped onto a CH46 Sea Knight, on orders from President Gerald Ford. The ambassador had lost his only son in the war, killed in combat. To the very end, he tried to support South Vietnam.

Once the ambassador was on board, the Sea Knight lifted into the sky, its lights doused to avoid enemy fire.

The helicopter pilot called the flagship of Task Force 76, waiting off shore, with the 46 vessels of the 7th Fleet.

Mission accomplished: he was carrying the ambassador whose code name was "TIGER."

More than 400 Vietnamese waiting their turn on the embassy grounds could not be saved.

In all, 1400 Westerners and 5,600 Vietnamese were airlifted out on 80 helicopters that flew 700 missions in 24 hours.

TCHOFF

TCHOFF

Budweiser beer can

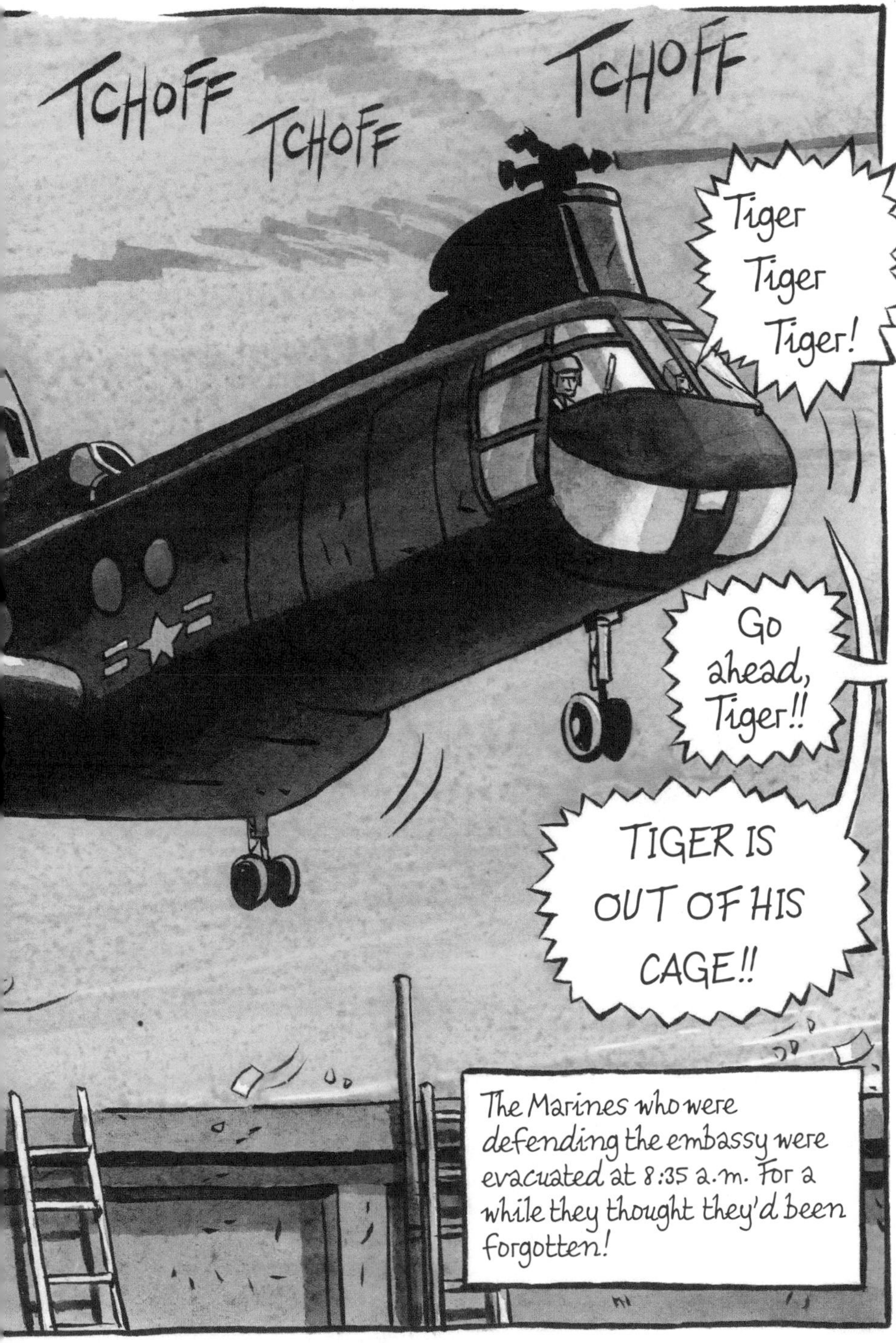
TCHOFF
TCHOFF
TCHOFF
Tiger Tiger Tiger!
Go ahead, Tiger!!
TIGER IS OUT OF HIS CAGE!!
The Marines who were defending the embassy were evacuated at 8:35 a.m. For a while they thought they'd been forgotten!

As April 30 dawned, North Vietnamese troops moved into the city. The people of Saigon laid low in their houses. Certain units of the South still put up resistance. Others put down their weapons and took off their uniforms and melted into the city. The situation was untenable. At 10:24 a.m., last-minute President Duong Van Minh ordered the troops to lay down their weapons and waited for the Communists to take over. At 11:30, two tanks from the North smashed through the gates of the Presidential Palace. It was the end. That very evening, Saigon was renamed Hô Chi Minh City.

And so Vietnam was reunified, but it was not "a peaceful, step-by-step process" as promised,* but through the brute force of a lightning offensive.

We lost many comrades in the fighting around Saigon!

Thanks to your sacrifice, victory is ours.

RPG

Method of peaceful reunification: the T54 Soviet tank (36.5 tons, 100-mm cannon, and two machine guns)

*Lê Duc Tho, January 24, 1973, in Paris.

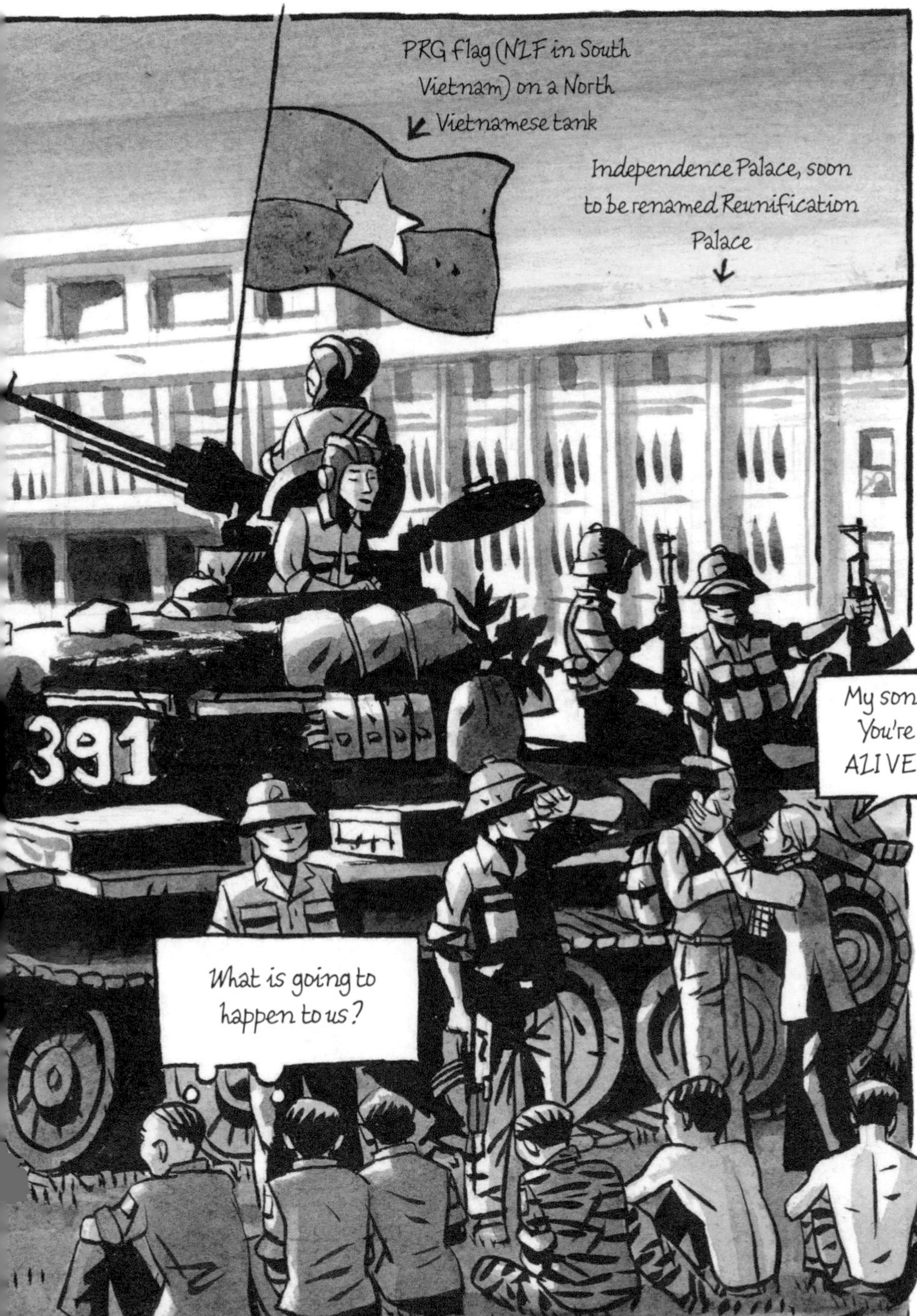
PRG flag (NLF in South Vietnam) on a North Vietnamese tank
Independence Palace, soon to be renamed Reunification Palace
391
My son! You're ALIVE!
What is going to happen to us?
South Vietnamese prisoners

As early as April 29, thousands of Vietnamese, left behind by the airlift, fled by sea on fishing boats, junks, and makeshift craft. They were picked up by ships of Task Force 76, part of the 7th Fleet. Civilian freighters joined in the rescue.

TCHOFF TCHOFF TCHOFF TCHOFF TCHOFF

NAVY "O O"

Task Force 76, 7th Fleet

← Boat people →

This exodus by sea was only the beginning. Three million Vietnamese risked their lives on the ocean starting in 1975. It is estimated that at least 250,000 boat people perished. Theft and rape at the hands of pirates was the lot of many escapees.

S.O.S.

CHILDREN OF THE LIBERATION

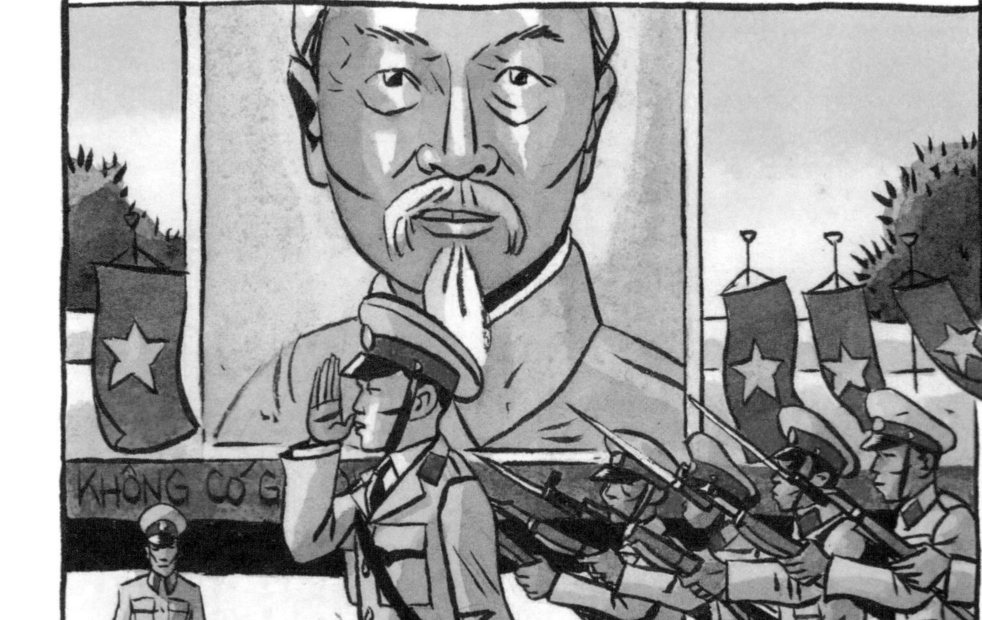
KHÔNG CÓ
Goose step
Vanilla-colored uniforms, "vani" in Vietnamese
CLOMP CLOMP CLOMP

"One rapid but fairly sure guide to the social atmosphere of a country is the parade-step of its army." – George Orwell, "England Your England"

Sadness, worry, and uncertainty were my companions during the month of May 1975, following the fall of Saigon. The year-end exams at Sciences Po were approaching. One candidate out of two would be refused, and I had plenty of holes in my knowledge.

Anxious about our family in Vietnam, I called Papa at work. He was receiving information through a wide network of Vietnamese family and friends from the diaspora. The Indochina wars had exiled people to the four corners of the earth.

Hmm, what if I presented this book at the history oral? Bernard Fall wrote it here!

"The Viêt-Minh Regime," Bernard Fall, 1960

At least your Uncle Diên is safe in the US with his family. One less worry!*

Let's wait and see what the new regime will do.

Maybe they will succeed where we failed because of the war!

LET'S GIVE THEM A CHANCE!

* Trương Bửu Điện was South Vietnam's Minister of Information in 1975.

268

We lived in a constant state of waiting. News from Vietnam was rare. Like Cambodia, but less hermetic, Vietnam hid behind a bamboo curtain. Western journalists headed for other hunting grounds. Beirut replaced Saigon on page one of the papers.

Má* said she received the money order, and Marco's package---
(Papa goes silent)

Anh-Noëlle, at 15

My God, it's so sad!

The sewing needles and fasteners sell well – by the piece – at the market.

A stamp for an overseas letter is a day's work!!

Later, in a Parisian post office

What have you got in your package?

Uh--- Safety pins, sewing needles, snap fasteners, hooks --- Elastic ribbon --- For Vietnam!

Ah, VIETNAM! Our Asian comrades! FREE AT LAST!!

How much, please?

??!!

*Mama

269

There was no outright blood bath, but a discreet social cleansing was carried out after the Communist victory. Suicides, disappearances, and executions eliminated a certain number of "enemies of the people," as the new regime's adversaries were called. The fate of the "petty bourgeois" from the old regime? Slow asphyxiation, for they had been judged to be reactionaries (phản động*). VAE VICTIS – woe to the vanquished.

former government worker, executive in private industry, intellectual, or merchant under the "puppet" regime

*Phản Động: traitor, reactionary.

The NLF had promised to respect basic freedoms many times before 1975, but all that changed. The rule of law did not exist. Local wardens – often former domestics – ran the show in the name of the Party.

Shit! What right *does* he have to do that?!

Say goodbye to your *decadent* Yankee hairstyle!

local warden ➚

Fear ruled society. Anyone who owned foreign objects that betrayed bourgeois tastes or acquaintanceship with the West quickly got rid of them.

I'd better cut off the labels on my French clothes!

The Vietnamese Communists were fully aware of the power of Western media. During the war, they reveled at the way the newspapers and TV criticized the Saigon regime. The taming of the South was carried out carefully. "Beat your dog behind closed doors!" was the advice of the Maoist Chinese Big Brother.

NO! NO PHOTOS!

What was to be done with all the "enemies of the people"? Eliminate them? That was often done — quietly, of course — but doing so meant losing a source of cheap labor. It was better to imprison them for indeterminate sentences in reeducation camps ---

The former puppets had to write down their own confessions. They rewrote them once, a hundred times, a thousand times, until they were judged "sincere" by the can bô.*

* Cấn bộ : Party cadres.

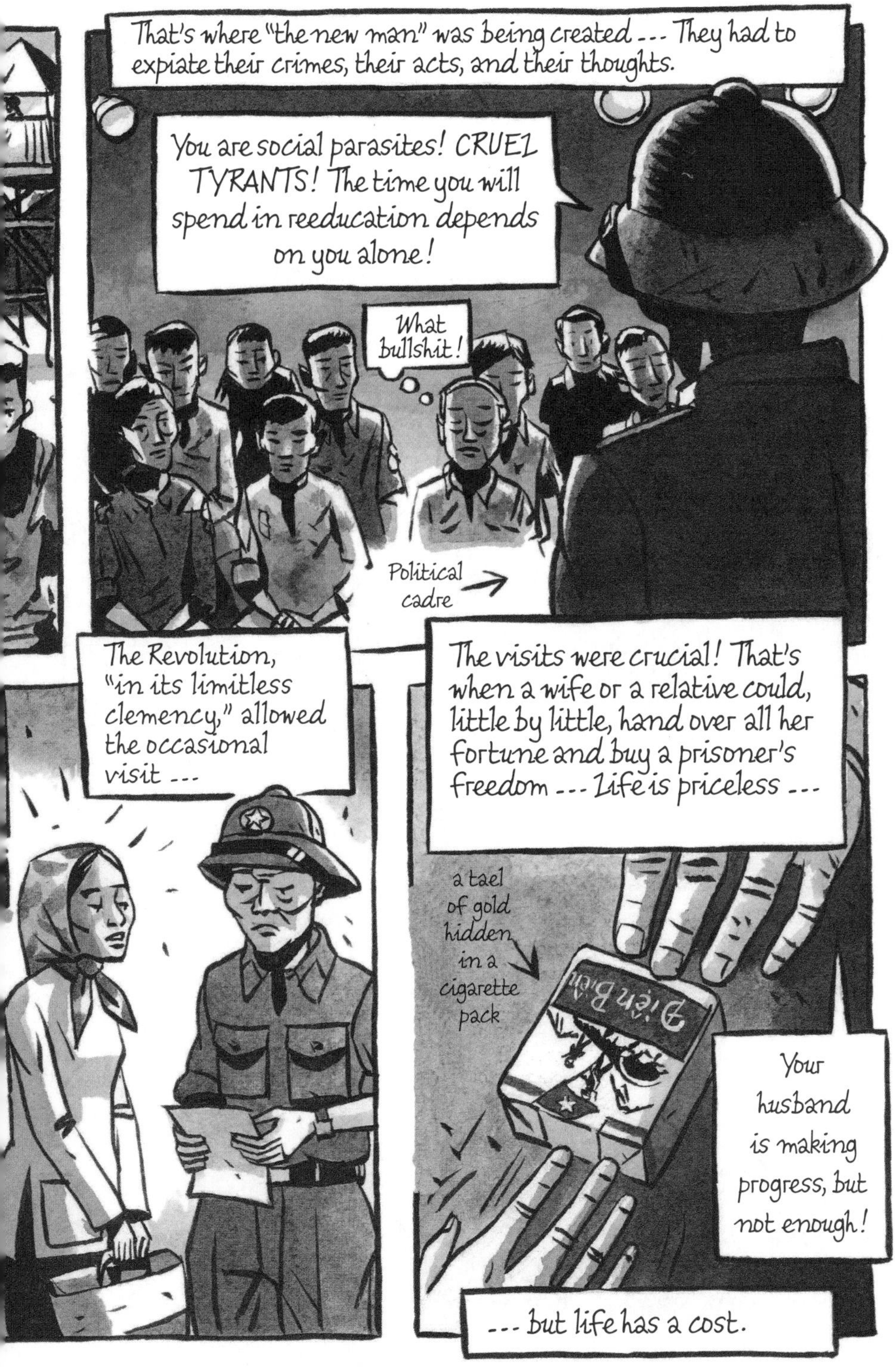
That's where "the new man" was being created --- They had to expiate their crimes, their acts, and their thoughts.
You are social parasites! CRUEL TYRANTS! The time you will spend in reeducation depends on you alone!
What bullshit!
Political cadre
The Revolution, "in its limitless clemency," allowed the occasional visit ---
The visits were crucial! That's when a wife or a relative could, little by little, hand over all her fortune and buy a prisoner's freedom --- Life is priceless ---
a tael of gold hidden in a cigarette pack
Your husband is making progress, but not enough!
--- but life has a cost.

The West didn't see much of these Asian concentration camps. Pictures of the camps were exceedingly rare, and these days, "no photos" means "it doesn't exist." Many Vietnamese gulags were bamboo structures built by the prisoners and destroyed afterward to eliminate the past. All that's left are survivors' stories. It is estimated that between 1 and 2.5 million Vietnamese were interned without due process for periods of up to 19 years. Of the ▨ incarcerated, 165,000 died in the camps.

After 1975, the boat people's ocean journey into uncertainty was the part of the Vietnamese iceberg that the West could see. The first large-scale exodus – a semi-official system in itself – was that of the ethnic Chinese of Vietnam, between 1978 and 1980. Thousands of them, often merchants, were cast into exile after being stripped of their possessions. After the South was defeated, the conquerors went into racketeering.

During the war, the Communists missed no chance to proclaim they were peace-loving, but three years after their victory, the country was involved in two bloody conflicts against former allies: the Khmer Rouge in Cambodia, and the People's Republic of China.

In 1978, to avenge the massacres perpetrated by the Khmer Rouge against Vietnamese populations in the border zone, Hanoi sent an army of 150,000 bộ đội,* mainly recruited from young men in the South.

MOVE UP!

AAAAAAAH

Show them you've got guts!!

Soldier with RPG

battle-hardened NCO

The Khmer Rouge were pushed back to the Thai border and the Vietnamese occupied Cambodia for the next ten years.

In 1979, wanting to teach their neighbors to the south a lesson since they had attacked their Khmer Rouge protégés, China crossed the Vietnamese border with 150,000 men and 500 tanks. But the Chinese were stopped.

We crushed the Chinese, but at such a high price!!

Yes, but we will never divulge our losses. Sun Tzu said, "All warfare is based on deception"!

*Bộ đội soldier of the People's Army of Vietnam.

275

The reunified country had been shaken by war, but the Communist Party imposed a brutal collectivization plan on the South, whose economy had been flourishing even before American aid, and despite the conflict. Collectivization was a spectacular failure, and by 1985, famine threatened. Turning to its enemy and brother China, which ten years earlier had successfully converted to the market economy, socialist Vietnam did the same, dropping the bombastic declarations of the past with its virulent attacks on capitalism. "Đổi mới"* was proclaimed in 1986, but economic growth and the opening of the country to large-scale tourism have not led to the easing of political constraints. Power is the monopoly of a single Party that accepts no pluralism, and no opposition. The population has been invigorated by the move to a market economy, but the Party continues to dominate.

*Đổi mới: "Renovation"

276

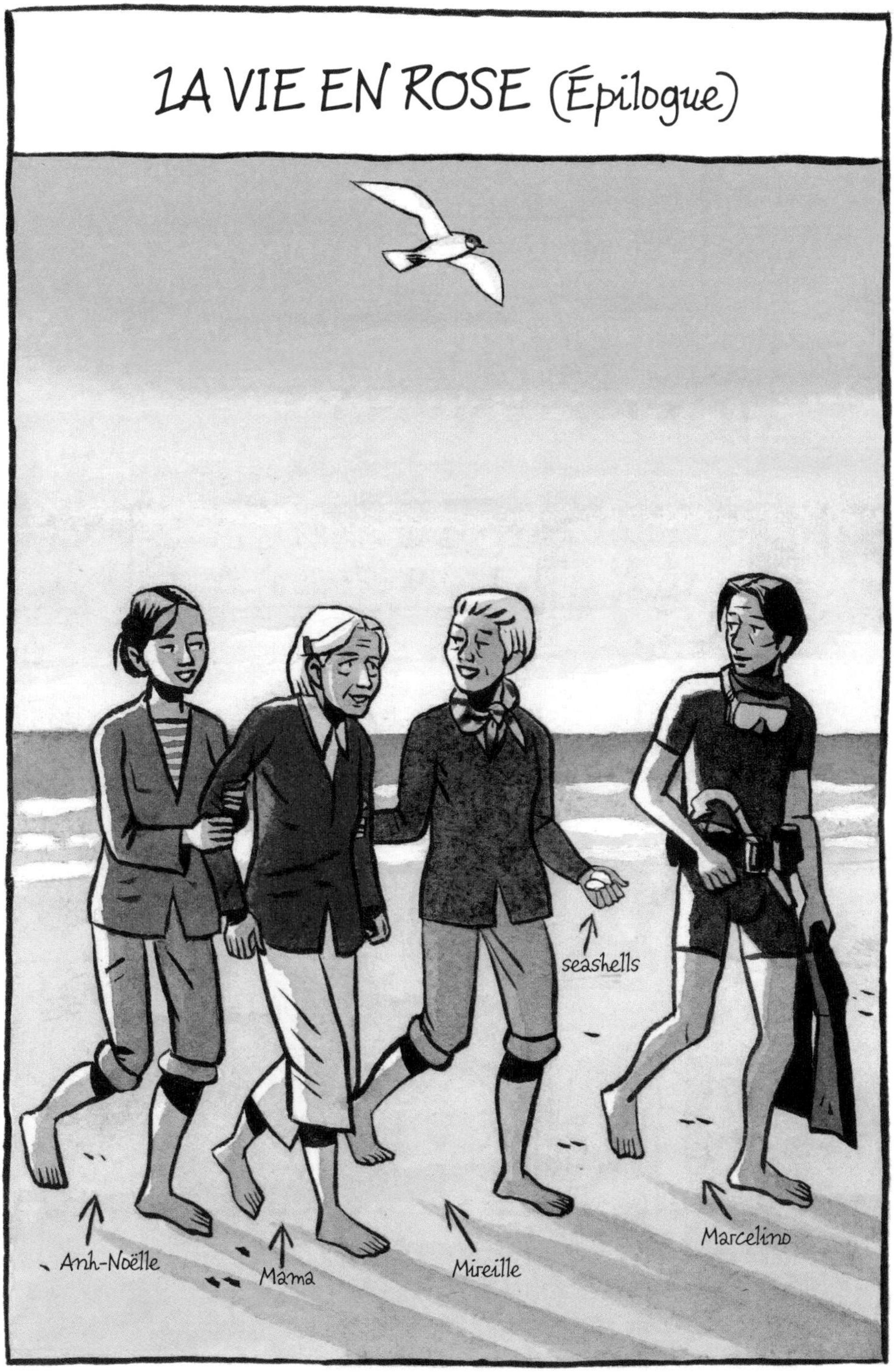
LA VIE EN ROSE (Épilogue)
seashells
Anh-Noëlle
Mama
Mireille
Marcelino

Before Mama left us to mourn in 2015, when the weather was mild, we would take her for walks along the beach where she played as a little girl. Two members of the Truong clan were missing. Papa passed away in 2012, to our great sadness. Dominique went thirty-six years earlier, much too soon.

In 1979, hitchhiking back from a stay in his community in Pune, India, Dominique stopped off in the city of Orange in southern France. He climbed up to the roof of a tall building in the suburbs, and Dominique – alias Swami Ramamurti – launched himself toward the far shore…

Orange was the color worn in the Pune ashram. My brother Swami Ramamurti used to say it was also the color of rebirth, of REINCARNATION.

Maybe Dominique came back as a seagull. Those birds seem so free. And Papa might be a bird too, a prince of the clouds ---

In her last years, Mama found a measure of peace in her new residence. She was living in a cloud, and that was just fine.

Tomorrow there's a tea dance at the residence, Mama.

Oh, really? How nice!

It'll be just like the disco, Mama.

It was easy to make Mama smile. You just had to take her hand, tell her a joke, or sing her a song. She loved chocolate too.

FIN

  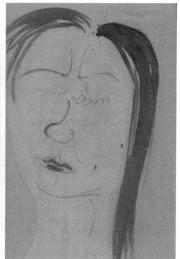

I would like to thank my publisher at Denoël, Jean-Luc Fromental, for the total freedom of expression he gave me as I worked on this project with a polemical theme and an often painful story.

My thanks also go to my family, my friends, and to all those who became my partners by telling me of their own experiences as I worked on this long journey: Yvette Truong, Mireille-Mai Truong, Anh-Noëlle Truong, Jeanne Thanh, Pham Van Tin, Ségolène Pham, Lignon Nguyên Thi Truoc, Tôn Nu Thuy Lan, Clémence Préaux, Yves Heck, Vincent Ton Van, Do Kh., Pham Ngoc Lân, Hong My Basray, Cécile Truong, Malou Vu Van, Anne-Laure Pham, Quang Quang, Luan Ly, Paloma Truong, Capucine Truong, Prune Truong, Truong Huu Luong, Christian Préaud, Nagi Baz, Odile Leduc, Cao Thuong Nga, Andrée Sang, Lucien Trong, Lê Thi Hiên Minh, Truong Buu Lâm, Nathalie Nguyên Huynh Châu, Richard Botterill, Pierre Brocheux, Hélène Gédouin, Nicolas Thai Hoang Nguyen, Gérard Lo Monaco, Katie Fechtmann, and many others ...

Marcelino Truong Luc

Mireille as a child, seen by Mama
Domi seen by Mireille
Mireille, self-portrait

Photo: Bastien Ortola

Marcelino Truong is an illustrator, painter, and author. Born the son of a Vietnamese diplomat in 1957 in the Philippines, he and his family moved to America (where his father worked for the embassy) and then to Vietnam at the outset of the war. He attended the French Lycee in London, then moved to Paris where he earned degrees in law at the Paris Institute of Political Studies, and English literature at the Sorbonne. Marcelino's first graphic memoir, *Such a Lovely Little War: Saigon 1963-65*, was published in French by Editions Denoël in 2012, and in English by Arsenal Pulp Press in 2016.

David Homel (translator) is a writer, journalist, filmmaker, and translator. His most recent novel is *The Fledglings* (Cormorant Books). He has translated many French-language books, including Marcelino Truong's *Such a Lovely Little War*, and is a two-time Governor General's Literary Award winner. He lives in Montreal.